ENDORSEMENTS

"Calling all men and women — especially those who are preparing for marriage or have been married for many years!! I found a book that must be read together. *"The Diamond in Your Household of Faith"* is a thorough marriage relationship manual. Well researched and well written, Dr. Weeter has produced a book that lifts the women to the place where God wants them to be—and instructs the men how to help the Lord get that done. After being married for over forty years, I was inspired with fresh revelation of how to encourage and be a true support to my wife.

Here is a book that women have been praying for—and men need to read! Guys, some of you have been frustrated in your marriage. You gripe about your wife and don't know what to do about it. Well, here is the answer. Read this book and you will find out the secret to a healthy, amazing marriage!"

PASTOR GEORGE PEARSONS

Eagle Mountain International Church

The Diamond in Your Household of Faith Study Guide

ISBN: 978-1-7341832-2-1

Copyright © 2021 David Weeter Ministries
P.O. Box 156
Haslet, TX 76052

Front cover image by Brian Duffield.

First printing, 2020.

Contact@DavidWeeter.org

The Diamond

IN YOUR
HOUSEHOLD
OF FAITH

Dr. David Weeter

INTRODUCTION

After so many great reviews from Pastors and teachers and receiving their requests for an accompanying workbook for our newest book, Lynn and I are very pleased to bring to you this companion study guide for *The Diamond in Your Household of Faith*!

Our approach to this dynamic study combination of book and workbook is much as marriage should be—complementary! While I was the primary author of the book (with Lynn offering input and suggestions), Lynn was the primary author of the workbook which includes questions and topics of discussion, with my input and suggestions. We feel as though this approach has produced the type of in-depth study material suitable for use in pre-marital counseling, marriage counseling, and general small group studies that our Pastoral friends have requested.

Presented in a simple, chapter-by-chapter format, this is a practical resource that will guide you through the book, *The Diamond in Your Household of Faith*. The study's guide utilizes simple fill-in-the-blank questions and broader reflection and discussion questions designed to provoke God-inspired thoughts and action steps you can take to put these powerful truths into action in your marriage. It also includes space at the end of the study guide to record your personal, targeted faith confessions. Additionally, there is an "Answer Key" at the back of the study guide.

The Diamond in Your Household of Faith is by no means an exhaustive work on marriage; however, it does contain a specific revelation from the Word—a revelation that addresses a misconception prevalent in Christian marriages that we have observed all of our lives. This simply profound connection the Lord revealed to us in His Word answers questions we have been asked throughout our more than 30 years of marriage, and it will answer questions for you!

It is our desire that as couples read, study and apply the truths contained in *The Diamond in Your Household of Faith,* they will become the unshakeable, unbreakable, and overcoming force that God intended! Once the couple becomes that force, the family will follow. And once families become that force, then the church will be unstoppable, because the church is made up of families!

Lynn and I join our faith with yours for the manifestation of 1 Peter 3:7 so you enjoy the grace of life together and that your prayers be not hindered in the slightest! In fact, that is the purpose of David Weeter Ministries—to teach real people how to have real faith in a real God to achieve real victory, in every area of life!

CHAPTER 1
THE DIAMOND

◇ GEMSTONES

Gemstones is a term that denotes a group of four gems: diamond, emerald, sapphire and ruby. To this day, diamonds are the most valuable, precious gems of all of the gemstones.

When it comes to durability, diamond is the undisputed winner over most gemstones. Very few gems come even close to it in terms of hardness.

1. God created diamonds as examples of extreme _____ combined with extreme_____.

2. A diamond's value, preciousness and rarity are _____ _____ _____.

3. Read Proverbs 31:10 (in the *Amplified Bible Classic*)
   What does it have to say about the value of a virtuous woman?
   _____

Amplified Bible Classic says it this way, "A capable, intelligent, and virtuous woman—who is he who can find her? She is far more precious than jewels and her value is far above rubies or pearls."

4. The _____ _____ is the _____ in your household of faith.

5. If the value of a diamond is far above the value of all the other gemstones, we can infer the diamond is _____ _____ the other gems.

Read Isaiah 54:11-12 in the *Amplified Bible Classic*

O you afflicted [city], storm-tossed and not comforted, behold, I will set your stones in fair colors [in antimony to enhance their brilliance] and lay your foundations with sapphires.

[12] And I will make your windows and pinnacles of [sparkling] agates *or* rubies, and your gates of [shining] carbuncles, and all your walls [of your enclosures] of precious stones.

6. When it says foundations, windows, gates and walls, what is it referring to?

    _____

7. What is the master gem in your household? Your_____.

8. The Lord furnishes your diamond with _____ to build a household.

Your home and your family are designed, built and equipped with each of these gems, and the diamond is set at the top.

◈ THE SETTING

1. There are two primary purposes for the setting. What is the first one?

    _____

Because of the many facets of a high-quality diamond, the setting is important to the appearance of the diamond. The facets affect the reflection and refraction of light…

2. What does "in antimony to enhance their brilliance" mean?

    _____

3. The second purpose of a jewel's setting is a _____ _____.

4. The appropriate setting keeps the stone_____ in its _____.

◈ PROPER PLACE IN THE HOME

1. The results of the diamond being in its proper setting is in Isaiah 54:13.
    What does it say happens when the stones and gems are in their place?

    _____

    _____

Note: Verse 13 begins with the conjunction "and." A conjunction takes what comes before it and connects it with what follows. Therefore, when the stones and gems are in their place, when the diamond is brilliantly and securely set, when the foundations, windows, gates, walls, and borders are laid with their gemstones, *then* all of your children shall be taught of the Lord and be obedient to His will. *Then* great shall be the peace and undisturbed composure of your children. *Because* you establish yourself in righteousness, you will be far from even the thought of oppression or destruction at that time, for you shall not fear, and terror shall not come near you.

2. What setting will enhance the diamond's _____ and keep it

    _____?

3. In other words, what is the proper place in the _____ for the

    _____?

Read Ephesians 1:22, 5:23-29

4. Due to the natural order in the physical realm on this earth, the _____ is

    placed as the _____ and _____ of his _____.

5. What does "head" mean in that verse? _____, _____,

    _____

6. As we study, it becomes that the wife is at the head of the _____ of

    the _____.

7. Essentially a family is an institution of humans that has to be _____.

People like to think that a "loving family" only needs its members to love one another and everything else will fall into place. That may be partially true. Love is the power that makes everything work.

8. Because of the multitude of _____ _____ in a family that

    need to be dealt with, a wife must be _____.

The most desirable and valuable diamonds—including the one in your household—are multi-faceted to provide maximum *light* return!

As you continue this study, keep this principle of the multifaceted cut in mind.

GEMS FOR REFLECTION AND APPLICATION

Answer each question and then discuss with each other. Make a corresponding action plan to accomplish these things. Recheck your action plan monthly to see if you are on target. If not, adjust and keep going. *The only way you fail is if you quit.*

The two purposes of the setting are: to show off the diamond and to provide security.

MEN

What are the qualities you want others to see in your wife?

_____

_____

_____

_____

_____

WOMEN:

What are the qualities you would like others to see in you?

_____

_____

_____

_____

_____

MEN:

What do you think you can do to make your wife feel secure?

_____

_____

_____

_____

_____

WOMEN:

What can your husband do to make you feel secure?

_____

_____

_____

_____

_____

FINAL THOUGHT:

Do your kids have peace and composure? If not, check your setting.

_____

_____

_____

_____

_____

_____

CHAPTER 1

NOTES

_____

_____

_____

_____

_____

_____

_____

_____

_____

_____

_____

_____

_____

_____

_____

_____

_____

_____

_____

_____

_____

_____

_____

_____

_____

_____

_____

_____

_____

_____

_____

_____

_____

_____

_____

_____

_____

_____

_____

_____

_____

_____

_____

_____

CHAPTER 2

THE PROVERBS 31 WOMAN

◈ WHAT DO MOST THINK IT MEANS TO BE A VIRTUOUS WOMAN?

Proverbs 31:10-31 *KJV*

¹⁰ Who can find a virtuous woman? for her price is far above rubies.

¹¹ The heart of her husband doth safely trust in her, so that he shall have no need of spoil.

¹² She will do him good and not evil all the days of her life.

¹³ She seeketh wool, and flax, and worketh willingly with her hands.

¹⁴ She is like the merchants' ships; she bringeth her food from afar.

¹⁵ She riseth also while it is yet night, and giveth meat to her household, and a portion to her maidens.

¹⁶ She considereth a field, and buyeth it: with the fruit of her hands she planteth a vineyard.

¹⁷ She girdeth her loins with strength, and strengtheneth her arms.

¹⁸ She perceiveth that her merchandise is good: her candle goeth not out by night.

¹⁹ She layeth her hands to the spindle, and her hands hold the distaff.

²⁰ She stretcheth out her hand to the poor; yea, she reacheth forth her hands to the needy.

²¹ She is not afraid of the snow for her household: for all her household are clothed with scarlet.

²² She maketh herself coverings of tapestry; her clothing is silk and purple.

²³ Her husband is known in the gates, when he sitteth among the elders of the land.

²⁴ She maketh fine linen, and selleth it; and delivereth girdles unto the merchant.

²⁵ Strength and honour are her clothing; and she shall rejoice in time to come.

²⁶ She openeth her mouth with wisdom; and in her tongue is the law of kindness.

²⁷ She looketh well to the ways of her household, and eateth not the bread of idleness.

²⁸ Her children arise up, and call her blessed; her husband also, and he praiseth her.

²⁹ Many daughters have done virtuously, but thou excellest them all.

³⁰ Favour is deceitful, and beauty is vain: but a woman that feareth the Lord, she shall be praised.

³¹ Give her of the fruit of her hands; and let her own works praise her in the gates.

1. What are some words the majority of the body of Christ uses to describe a "virtuous" woman?

    _____

    _____

2. Which language was used to write the book of Proverbs? _____

3. Read 2 Samuel 23

4. The word "virtuous" (chayil—Strong's H2428) in Proverbs 31 is the same as which word in 2 Samuel 23? _____

5. What does the word "Chayil" mean in Hebrew?

    "a _____, whether of men, means or other resources; an _____,

    _____, _____, _____, _____,

    _____, activity, army, a band of soldiers, or a company; great forces, goods,

    host, might, power, riches, strength, strong, substance, train as in training of a soldier,

    valiant, valor, virtuous, war, and worthy."

❖ How God Describes This Virtuous Woman

Let's go through Proverbs 31 and see how God describes the details of this virtuous woman. It's no wonder her price is far above rubies; it's no wonder she is the diamond.

1. vv11-12 "The heart of her husband doth safely trust in her, so that he shall have no need of spoil. She will do him good and not evil all the days of her life"

    a. You can _____ someone who is _____ and full of _____ and _____.

    b. This virtuous woman is _____.

2. vv 13-14 "She seeks wool, and flax, and works willingly with her hands. She is like the merchants' ships; she brings her food from afar"

    _____ _____ the Proverbs 31 woman has the means, resources, and ability to do these things.

3. v. 16 "She considers a field and buys it: with the fruit of her hands she plants a vineyard"

    How is she able to do these things?

    She is _____, _____ and _____.

4. v. 17 "She girds her loins with strength and strengthens her arms."

    She is _____ and is not _____ of anything.

5. v. 18 "She perceives that her merchandise is good."

    She makes _____ _____ and does things with _____.

6. v. 20 "She stretches out her hand to the poor"

    She gives _____ to the poor.

7. vv. 21–22 "All her household are clothed with scarlet. She makes herself coverings of tapestry; her clothing is silk and purple"

    In the context of the day, these were _____, _____ articles.

8. v. 23 "Her husband is known in the gates, when he sits among the elders of the land"

   This is the description of the _____ _____ as
   God intended.

9. v. 24 "She makes fine linen and sells it"

   She knows how to _____ a _____.

10. vv. 24–25 "She delivers girdles unto the merchant. Strength and honor are her clothing"

    Her fashion style is her own, based on _____ and _____.

11. v. 26 "She opens her mouth with wisdom; and in her tongue is the law of kindness"

    The virtuous woman can speak a word from God in your life and _____
    _____.

12. v. 28 "She looks well to the ways of her household and eats not the bread of idleness. Her
    children arise up, and call her blessed; her husband also, and he praises her"

    Her husband lifts her up and _____ her! He doesn't _____
    or _____ her.

13. v. 29 "Many daughters have done virtuously, but thou excel them all"

    These are the daughters taught by a virtuous woman. Elder women are to
    _____ the _____ according to the book of Titus.
    (See Titus 2:3–4).

14. vv. 29–30 "Favor is deceitful, and beauty is vain: but a woman that fears the Lord, she
    shall be praised. Give her of the fruit of her hands; and let her own works praise her in
    the gates"

    Not only will the virtuous woman who fears the Lord have _____
    _____, but she shall also be praised.

15. One of the attributes of a diamond that determines its value is a multifaceted cut. It is
    no coincidence that Proverbs 31 seems to be describing some sort of Wonder
    Woman superhero!

    She is _____ and therefore _____ _____.

⬦ GEMS FOR REFLECTION AND APPLICATION ⬦

Answer each question and then discuss. Make a corresponding action plan to accomplish these things. Recheck your action plan monthly to see if you are on target. If not, adjust and keep going. *The only way you fail is if you quit.*

BOTH:

What are modern day equivalents to each verse?

_____

_____

_____

_____

_____

_____

_____

_____

_____

_____

MEN:

How can you help your wife step out in any of these areas?

_____

_____

_____

_____

WOMEN:

How can you implement improvement or stepping out in any of these areas?

_____

_____

_____

_____

BOTH:

How would these items change what your family looks/acts like? The family dynamics?

_____

_____

_____

_____

_____

_____

_____

_____

_____

CHAPTER 2
NOTES

_____

_____

_____

_____

_____

_____

_____

_____

_____

_____

_____

_____

_____

_____

_____

_____

_____

_____

_____

_____

_____

CHAPTER 3

THE REST OF THE STORY

In addition to Proverbs 31, God specifically addresses a woman in Isaiah 54.

Isaiah 54:1-17 *KJV*

> Sing, O barren, thou that didst not bear; break forth into singing, and cry aloud, thou that didst not travail with child: for more are the children of the desolate than the children of the married wife, saith the Lord. ² Enlarge the place of thy tent, and let them stretch forth the curtains of thine habitations: spare not, lengthen thy cords, and strengthen thy stakes;
>
> ³ For thou shalt break forth on the right hand and on the left; and thy seed shall inherit the Gentiles, and make the desolate cities to be inhabited. ⁴ Fear not; for thou shalt not be ashamed: neither be thou confounded; for thou shalt not be put to shame: for thou shalt forget the shame of thy youth, and shalt not remember the reproach of thy widowhood any more.⁵ For thy Maker is thine husband; the Lord of hosts is his name; and thy Redeemer the Holy One of Israel; The God of the whole earth shall he be called.
>
> ⁶ For the Lord hath called thee as a woman forsaken and grieved in spirit, and a wife of youth, when thou wast refused, saith thy God. ⁷ For a small moment have I forsaken thee; but with great mercies will I gather thee. ⁸ In a little wrath I hid my face from thee for a moment; but with everlasting kindness will I have mercy on thee, saith the Lord thy Redeemer. ⁹ For this is as the waters of Noah unto me: for as I have sworn that the waters of Noah should no more go over the earth; so have I sworn that I would not be wroth with thee, nor rebuke thee. ¹⁰ For the mountains shall depart, and the hills be removed; but my kindness shall not depart from thee, neither shall the covenant of my peace be removed, saith the Lord that hath mercy on thee. ¹¹ O thou afflicted, tossed with tempest, and not comforted, behold, I will lay thy stones with fair colours, and lay thy foundations with sapphires. ¹² And I will make thy windows of agates, and thy gates of carbuncles, and

all thy borders of pleasant stones. ¹³ And all thy children shall be taught of the Lord; and great shall be the peace of thy children. ¹⁴ In righteousness shalt thou be established: thou shalt be far from oppression; for thou shalt not fear: and from terror; for it shall not come near thee. ¹⁵ Behold, they shall surely gather together, but not by me: whosoever shall gather together against thee shall fall for thy sake. ¹⁶ Behold, I have created the smith that bloweth the coals in the fire, and that bringeth forth an instrument for his work; and I have created the waster to destroy. ¹⁷ No weapon that is formed against thee shall prosper; and every tongue that shall rise against thee in judgment thou shalt condemn. This is the heritage of the servants of the Lord, and their righteousness is of me, saith the Lord.

1. Let's look at some specific verses in this chapter.

    Vs. 1

    "Sing, O barren, thou that didst not bear; break forth into singing, and cry aloud, thou that didst not travail with child."

    Vs. 6

    "For the Lord has called thee as a woman forsaken and grieved in spirit, and a wife of youth, when thou wast refused, saith thy God."

    a. The woman described in Isaiah 54 has experienced a great amount of

    _____ and _____.

    b. Even as a young wife, she was _____.

2. Vs. 8

    "with everlasting kindness will I have mercy on thee, saith the Lord thy Redeemer"

    The Lord has shown _____ and has _____ her.

3. Vs. 11

    She has been "afflicted, tossed with tempest, and not comforted".

    No matter what this woman has been through, the Lord can use her to _____ something _____!

◈ THE STONES

Isaiah 54:11-12 *AMPC*

O you afflicted [city], storm-tossed and not comforted, behold, I will set your stones in fair colors [in antimony to enhance their brilliance] and lay your foundations with sapphires. ¹² And I will make your windows *and* pinnacles of [sparkling] agates *or* rubies, and your gates of [shining] carbuncles, and all your walls [of your enclosures] of precious stones.

The word **stones** indicates "to build".

1. As the diamond in the household of faith, the _____ builds with the precious stones at the _____ _____.

2. The Lord will "set" them in such a way that it will show the world their _____ and _____.

◈ THE FOUNDATION

Referring to Isaiah 54:11

Foundations *(Strong's Concordance H3245)*

yâçad yaw-sad': "to sit down together, to consult, to establish, to instruct; ordain, to set, and make sure."

1. Diamonds are the _____ of their home.

2. Who established the diamond as such? _____

3. Who is laying the foundations of your family? _____

There are several components of every strong foundation and, in the case of our homes, one of the critical components listed as a part of the foundation is the sapphire for an extremely critical reason.

Sapphire *(Strong' Concordance* H5601)

çappîyr, sap-peer: "a gem used for scratching other substances." The root word (H5608) even means "to score or inscribe with a mark as a record; to declare."

4. The wife (diamond) is to _____ the foundations of the home by _____ the Word of God over them.

Read John Osteen story on page 20.

Demons tremble at homes in which the very foundations are inscribed with the Word of God.

5. Diamonds _____ their homes in the _____, keeping it off limits to the devil.

❖ THE WINDOWS

Vs. 12 "I will make your windows of agates, and thy gates of carbuncles"

Windows has several different meanings:
"brilliant; a ray" as in a ray of light;
"a notched battlement" which is a place in a fortress, notched out to wage battle.

Agate means "deep."

1. Your diamond should have _____, clear _____ for her family and the call of God on their lives.

2. The greater the clarity of the diamond, the _____ the _____.

3. This clarity of vision is a "notched space of battlement" through which to _____ all the _____ of the _____.

❖ THE GATES

Vs. 12....."and your gates of carbuncles."

Gate can mean:

"to act as a gate keeper."

"to estimate and to think."

1. The diamond is the _____ of your home.

2. How does the diamond act as gatekeeper?

    a. _____

    b. _____

    c. _____

    d. _____

3. Think about your household in these areas:

    a. _____

    b. _____

Carbuncle comes from two root words:

'eqdach meaning "a fiery gem," and *'eben* meaning "to build."

4. The idea of building the home is _____.

5. When the enemy is trying to gain access to your home, it is necessary to be a

    _____ _____.

❖ THE BORDERS

Referring to Isaiah 54:12

".....And all your borders of pleasant stones."

1. A border is "a boundary, a territory _____; to bound as with a _____."

2. And a three-stranded rope is not _____ _____. (See Ecc. 4:12.)

3. The three stranded rope includes _____, _____, _____

4. What is the border that will enclose your territory? _____

5. Mark your territory? _____.

❖ BUILDING EXCELLENCE

V. 13 And all thy children shall be taught of the Lord; and great shall be the peace of thy children

1. Once these things are in place and your home is built _____, these things shall take place.

2. Your home is established in _____.

3. _____, _____, and _____ shall not come near you because your home is built well.

Isaiah 54:17

No weapon that is formed against thee shall prosper; and every tongue that shall rise against thee in judgment thou shalt condemn. This is the heritage of the servants of the Lord, and their righteousness is of me, saith the Lord.

4. Be the _____ in your household of faith.

❖ WHO IS BUILDING YOUR HOME?

Psalm 127:1

"Except the Lord build the house."

1. The Lord is the _____.

2. He ordains everything for the _____ to be _____.

3. The "_____" handles all of the _____.

Proverbs 14:1

"Every wise woman buildeth her house."

4. _____ are the subcontractors.

5. They build the home using the _____ the _____ _____ has laid out.

Build *(Strong's Concordance* H1129)

bânâh, baw-naw'; "to build, to obtain children, to make, to *repair,* to set up."

(This is also the same word as "stones" in Isaiah 54:11)

6. Even if some things have gone wrong, God can and will _____ the household of faith.

7. When the diamond builds her house with the Master Builder, it is _____, _____ and _____.

Isaiah 48:13

Mine hand also hath laid the foundation of the earth, and my right hand hath spanned the heavens: when I call unto them, they stand up together.

Isaiah 51:13

… the Lord thy maker, that hath stretched forth the heavens, and laid the foundations of the earth

8. So where is the diamond's place in the _____ _____?

Isaiah 51:16

"I have put my words in your mouth, and I have covered thee in the shadow of my hand, that I may plant the heavens, and lay the foundations of the earth"

9. God gave us His Word as the _____ to _____ our _____.

❖ THE WHOLE PICTURE

Isaiah 54:11 "….He will lay the foundations with sapphires."

1. The sapphire is used to scratch other substances and to make a _____
    for record.

The Hebrew word *caphar* translated *sapphire* can also mean "talking about, declaring, speaking, and talking."

2. The wife lays the _____, marking the substances around the household
    by _____, **speaking,** _____, and _____.

What is she supposed to declare, speak, talk, and write?

3. The diamond _____ _____ _____ with the
    Father, _____ _____ _____, and she declares
    them, speaks them, talks about them, and marks her household off limits to Satan.

As you put this into action, the foundation of your household of faith will be strong and secure.

❖ ISAIAH 54 EXPANDED ❖

Putting together the definitions that we have read and what we have studied, I have written what we can call the Weeter Expanded Translation of these verses in Isaiah 54. Based on what we have studied, here is what I believe God is saying to the diamond through these verses in Isaiah 54:

> "You and I are going to sit down together and I am going to personally share My wisdom, insight and understanding with you. I am going to show you how to build the most beautiful and successful life and home that you can imagine. You will have to do the building but don't worry, I have the master plans and blueprints showing you exactly what to do every step of the way.

> "I will give you the words that you will use to lay the very foundations of your home, raise up the walls, and install the windows! You will use the power and authority in My words by declaring them to build impregnable gates and borders that no enemy can breach. I'll show you how to mark your territory. You will indelibly engrave your borders and gates with My mark with your declarations and then defend our territory with whatever firepower necessary to overcome any foe who would dare attempt to enter without your permission. I have equipped you with everything needed to build your home in such a manner to where it is an impenetrable fortress."

❦ GEMS FOR REFLECTION AND APPLICATION ❦

Answer each question and then discuss. Make a corresponding action plan to accomplish these things. Recheck your action plan monthly to see if you are on target. If not, adjust and keep going. *The only way you fail is if you quit.*

BOTH:

What practical steps can you take to help lay your foundation on the Word of God?

_____

_____

_____

_____

_____

_____

BOTH:

What are things you would like to repair in your relationship and family? What are some scriptures that you can use to pray in agreement over this? What are two or three action steps you can take to start on that repair?

_____

_____

_____

_____

_____

_____

CHAPTER 3
NOTES

CHAPTER 4
ONE WORD FROM GOD

The Word of God weaves pieces together and makes a fabric of truth.

1. Now that you have seen what the diamond of your household looks like, is a wife automatically this diamond? _____

2. How are these scriptures obtained and implemented?

   _____ _____

Proverbs 18:22

"Whoso findeth a wife findeth a good thing, and obtains favor of the Lord"

Proverbs 31:10

Who can find a virtuous woman?

3. Not every woman is _____.

4. Not every wife is a _____ _____.

Proverbs 25:24 *AMPC*

"It is better to dwell in the corner of the housetop than to share a house with a disagreeing, quarrelsome, and scolding woman.

Proverbs 21:9 *AMPC*

......nagging, quarrelsome, *and* faultfinding woman.

Good *(Strong's Concordance H2895)*

tôwb, tobe; "beautiful, best, better, bountiful, cheerful, at ease, fair, be in favor, fine, glad, gracious, joyful, kind, to be liked, to be loving, most pleasant, to be ready"

5. In _____ _____, the Lord shows the most wonderful, glorious description of the _____ of a _____.

6. Whoever finds a wife, finds a _____ _____.

Proverbs 19:14,

"House and riches are the inheritance of fathers: and a prudent wife is from the Lord."

Prudent *(Strong's Concordance* H7919)

sâkal, saw-kal; "intelligent, an expert, to instruct, to prosper; to deal prudently, skillful, to have good success, to teach, to have understanding and to make to understand."

7. A _____ wife is a _____ wife.

8. A prudent wife is _____ _____ _____.

❖ THE WORD WEAVES PIECES TOGETHER

This is where "all of your children shall be taught of the Lord and the elder woman shall teach the younger."

1. To have understanding or to make to understand is _____.

2. A prudent wife has wisdom to _____ and to be _____.

3. Grab ahold of these two characteristics by faith and become the diamond in your household of faith:

   a. _____

   b. _____

4. Implement these biblical descriptions by faith and you will become a _____.

Men, I don't see any possible way that you can read even a single paragraph of this book (with any sense whatsoever of the gift that God has given you) without an overwhelming sense of gratitude, thanksgiving, and value of this precious diamond with which the Lord God Almighty has blessed you.

❦ GEMS FOR REFLECTION AND APPLICATION ❦

Answer each question and then discuss. Make a corresponding action plan to accomplish these things. Recheck your action plan monthly to see if you are on target. If not, adjust and keep going. *The only way you fail is if you quit.*

MEN:

What are some of the good characteristics (strong points) you see in yourself?

_____

_____

_____

_____

What are some good characteristics (strong points) you see, and are thankful for, in your wife?

_____

_____

_____

_____

WOMEN:

What are some of your good characteristics or strong points?

_____

_____

_____

_____

What are some of the good characteristics (strong points) you see, and are thankful for, in your husband?

_____

_____

_____

_____

In this age of social media and Pinterest, we all have an idea of how to be "best" and "better," but let's focus on the terms "cheerful and at ease" in these scriptures. Just because someone else "hand makes" individual cookies for every child in their son's class, it doesn't mean that you should. Prudence helps us set those limits.

Are there any items that you have added to your lives that seemed like "good things" that did not add to your peace?

_____

_____

_____

_____

CHAPTER 4

NOTES

_____

_____

_____

_____

_____

_____

_____

_____

_____

_____

_____

_____

_____

_____

_____

_____

_____

_____

CHAPTER 5

YOUR NEW FILTER

We have discovered the true meanings of a virtuous woman, a good wife, and a prudent wife.

1. Keep these words with their full meanings as a _____ through which you read scriptures regarding wives.

2. What is the traditional way of thinking about women?

   _____, _____ , _____, _____,

   _____.

3. Don't let religious tradition _____ _____ and cause you to

   _____ _____ into the old traditional way of thinking.

4. _____ your _____, to the virtuous woman, the good wife, the prudent wife.

WIVES OF UNBELIEVING HUSBANDS

The topic of how she is to win over her husband for the Kingdom of God has also been misconstrued.

1 Peter 3:1

"Likewise, you wives, be in subjection to your own husbands; that, if any obey not the word, they also may without the word be won by the conversation of the wives."

1. The conversation of the wives can not only be how they talk— but also the manner of the wife's life.

2. The household is built by _____ and _____ the Word.

3. By her _____, _____, _____,

   _____, and _____

   to run the household well, responsibly, and efficiently, a virtuous, prudent and good wife is going to win over her unbelieving husband.

◆ ADORNMENT OF THE HEART

Let's look at one of the most misunderstood passages in the entire New Testament.

1 Peter 3:3–5

> "Whose adorning, let it not be that outward adorning of plaiting the hair, and of wearing of gold, or of putting on of apparel; but let it be the hidden man of the heart, in that which is not corruptible, even the ornament of a meek and quiet spirit, which is in the sight of God of great price. For after this manner in the old time the holy women also, who trusted in God, adorned themselves, being in subjection unto their own husbands."

Throughout our study in this book, our eyes have been opened and we have a new filter of how God says a wife is to be.

Weymouth Translation[1] of 1 Peter 3:3

> "Your adornment ought not to be a merely outward thing—one of plaiting the hair, putting on jewelry, or wearing beautiful dresses. Instead of that, it should be a new nature within— the imperishable ornament of a gentle and peaceful spirit, which is indeed precious in the sight of God."

1. _____ _____ is only one part; the _____ of the _____ _____ is also important to God.

v. 5

> "For in ancient times also this was the way the holy women who set their hopes upon God used to adorn themselves, being submissive to their husbands" (v. 5, Weymouth).

2. It is the wife's _____ to adorn herself in _____ to her own husband.

3. How she looks and what _____ _____ or _____ _____ is between the wife and her husband—and nobody else.

4. We have no right to _____ or _____ _____ someone else.

 1. Weymouth, Richard Francis. *Weymouth New Testament in Modern Speech*. Harrison House, 2012.

1 Peter 3:4

"But let it be the hidden man of the heart, in that which is not corruptible, even the ornament of a meek and quiet spirit, which is in the sight of God of great price."

5. The wife is "of _____ _____," or far more valuable than rubies or other gemstones.

6. She is indeed the _____ in your household of faith.

7. "Great price" can also mean " _____ _____."

8. She is of _____ _____ in the sight of God.

Reminder: We're talking about God, who has gold streets—not gold-plated streets but streets of pure gold. His front gate is not lined with pearls but made of pearl.

9. In God's eyes, even compared to streets of gold and pearl gates, your wife is of _____ _____.

10. A wife is _____ _____ _____ !

❧ GIVING HONOR TO

1 Peter 3:7

"Likewise, you husbands, dwell with them according to knowledge, giving honor unto the wife as unto the weaker vessel as being heirs together of the grace of life; that your prayers be not hindered."

1. A wife is not the _____ _____. She is _____ and _____.

2. A husband is to honor her _____ _____ she were a weaker vessel.

3. Giving her _____ means "to _____ as extremely costly and extremely pricey."

4. You have been given a _____ that God sees as extremely valuable and costly.

5. If you take that gift and _____ it with little to no _____, how do you expect your prayers to be fully active, powerful, or effective?

6. You must sit down _____ so that your prayers be not _____.

7. Husbands and wives are _____ _____ in the grace of life.

8. _____ who the diamond in your household of faith is.

9. Take a moment to acknowledge exactly how _____ and of _____ _____ a wife truly is in your life.

❤ GEMS FOR REFLECTION AND APPLICATION ❤

Answer each question and then discuss. Make a corresponding action plan to accomplish these things. Recheck your action plan monthly to see if you are on target. If not, adjust and keep going. *The only way you fail is if you quit.*

MEN:

How do you honor your wife? How do you DEMONSTRATE honor to your wife?

_____

_____

_____

_____

_____

_____

WOMEN:

What are some ways that you can improve your value to your husband?

_____

_____

_____

_____

_____

_____

CHAPTER 5

NOTES

———————————————————————————————————————

_____

_____

_____

_____

_____

_____

_____

_____

_____

_____

_____

_____

_____

_____

_____

_____

_____

_____

CHAPTER 6

TAKING IT TO THE
NEW TESTAMENT

We have looked at a lot of scriptures, definitions, and principles in the Old Testament, but do these truths carry over into the New Testament?

1. In the Old Testament who should build the house?

   _____ _____

2. In the New Testament we will see how the _____ _____ builds His house!

John 7:16

"Jesus answered them, and said, My doctrine is not mine, but his that sent me."

John 12:49–50

"For I have not spoken of myself; but the Father which sent me, he gave me a commandment, what I should say, and what I should speak. And I know that his commandment is life everlasting: whatsoever I speak therefore, even as the Father said unto me, so I speak."

The *Weymouth Translation* says, "I speak just as the Father has bidden me."

John 14:10

"Believest thou not that I am in the Father, and the Father in me? The words that I speak unto you I speak not of myself: but the Father that dwelleth in me, he doeth the works."

Weeter translation:

"I speak the Father's words and He does the works." The Chief Cornerstone of the household—Jesus—used the Father's words to build the Church—the house of God.

◈ BACK TO THE FOUNDATION

Ephesians 2:19–22 (italics added)

"Now therefore ye are no more strangers and foreigners, but fellow citizens with the saints, and of the household of God; And are built upon the *foundation* of the apostles and prophets,

Jesus Christ himself being the *chief corner stone;* In Whom all the building fitly framed together groweth unto a holy temple in the Lord: in whom ye also are builder together for a habitation of God through the Spirit"

1. This is the _____ _____ pattern—His _____.

2. It is how _____ operated, and how the _____ should operate.

3. As He speaks His words, the _____ does the work of laying the foundations of the home through the _____.

4. Another meaning of the word foundation in Ephesians 5 and Isaiah 54 is to _____ or to _____.

5. Satan has been able to rob the households of faith and the Church by _____ the _____ of the house away from being able to _____.

1 Corinthians 14:33

"For God is not the author of confusion, but of peace, as in all churches of the saints."

◆ WHO IS THE SCRIPTURE REFERRING TO?

1. The same Greek word translated as "women" also means "_____."

"For it is not permitted unto them to speak; but they are commanded to be under obedience as also saith the law. And if they will learn anything, let them ask their husbands at home: for it is a shame for women to speak in the church."

2. This verse is speaking about _____, so "woman" is referring to "_____."

Timothy 2:11,

"Let the woman learn in silence with all subjection. But I suffer not a woman to teach, or to usurp authority over the man, but to be in silence."

In some Christian denominations, women have not been allowed to teach, preach, or in some cases audibly pray in church based on these two scriptures.

The mindset of inequality, inferiority, and incompetence has carried over into the home and families of the household of faith.

3. It is important to take the time to _____, _____ and _____ what the words meant.

There are questions that need to be answered to rightly discern the scriptures.

- Was it talking about women or was it talking about wives?

- Was it talking about a particular church situation that was going on inside a particular culture or was it supposed to apply to all churches for all time in every situation?

Brother Kenneth E. Hagin wrote a book called *The Woman Question*. I encourage you to read his book on the subject as he clearly addresses, in detail, these scriptures as they apply to the woman's place in the church.

- Should she preach in the church?

- Should she teach in the church?

- Should she hold positions of authority in the church?

- How did all of these scriptures apply to the operation of the church itself and its function and leadership?

4. In Brother Hagin's book, *The Woman Question*,[2] the Law of _____ _____ is presented: *"By ignoring the law of interpretation, anyone can make scripture say anything you want them to say about anything. Every scripture must be interpreted in the light of what other scriptures have to say on the same subject. It must harmonize with all other scripture."*

This is what has happened with these two particular scriptures in 1 Corinthians 14 and 1 Timothy 2.

Let us review and discover scriptures that clearly support the fact that these have been grossly misinterpreted and incorrectly discerned causing much confusion instead of peace in the Church.

Proverbs 31:26

"She opens her mouth with wisdom."

5. In the *Strong's Concordance*, it shows that she speaks and teaches _____!

2. Hagin, Kenneth E. *The Woman Question.* Faith Library Publications, 1983.

6. The very nature of a virtuous woman includes not only _____ but also _____.

7. The Lord is the Master Builder and He builds the home through the _____.

8. He does the teaching _____ her.

Proverbs 19:14

"House and riches are the inheritance of fathers: and a prudent wife is from the Lord."

9. The definition of prudent includes the meaning " _____."

10. A prudent wife is to _____!

"When I call to remembrance the unfeigned faith that is in you, which dwelt first in your grandmother Lois, and your mother Eunice; and I am persuaded that in you also." Notice it doesn't say anything about Grandpa or Dad. It dwelt first in the grandmother then in the mother.

11. How does _____ come?

Romans 10:17

Faith comes by hearing and hearing by the Word of God.

12. That it is specifically the _____ _____—*rhema* in the Greek.

13. Timothy heard the _____ _____ of _____ from his grandmother and from his mother!

14. They taught him faith by speaking the Word to him.

❖ THE WORD SAYS WOMEN ARE SUPPOSED TO TEACH

Titus 2:1-4

"But speak thou the things which become sound doctrine: That the aged men be sober, grave, temperate, sound in faith, in charity, in patience. The aged women likewise, that they be in behaviour as becometh holiness, not false accusers, not given to much wine, *teachers* of good things; That they may teach the young women to be sober, to love their husbands, to love their children"

1. Scripture after scripture says that women are _____ to _____.

Luke 2:36-38

"And there was one Anna, a prophetess...and she was a widow of about fourscore and four years, which departed not from *the temple,* but she served God with fastings and prayers night and day. And she coming in that instant gave thanks likewise unto the Lord, and *spake of him* to all them that looked for redemption in Jerusalem"

2. Anna served God in the church, _____ to all who were looking for redemption.

3. A prophetess _____ the Word of the Lord.

Acts 18:26

"And [Apollos] began to speak boldly in the synagogue: whom when Aquila *and Priscilla* had heard, *they* took him unto them, and expounded unto him the way of God more perfectly"

4. Priscilla _____ and _____ the way of God to Apollos alongside her husband.

5. It is _____ for the diamond to teach and expound the things of God in the home and even outside of it.

6. As we saw in the word _____, it is an integral part of her _____.

◈ DIFFERENCES BETWEEN THE CULTURES

Greek and Roman Cultures

1. There is a _____ between Jewish women and the Gentiles to whom Paul preached.

2. With research, you'll find that the women in the Greek and Roman cultures were kept _____ _____.

3. Some women would _____ _____ out in the middle of the church service that had nothing to do with the service.

4. Paul had a systematical and organized approach to address the _____ _____ and achieve _____.

Jewish Culture

1. Every instance we have looked at in Scripture where the women were teaching and speaking the Word of the Lord, including the prophetess Anna and Timothy's mother and grandmother, are examples of _____ _____ .

2. The Jews _____ _____ keep their women ignorant.

3. They were _____ _____ in the scriptures.

4. Deborah in Judges 4 was a _____ as well as a _____.

5. She was a leader of the _____ _____ _____, obviously well-learned, as were all Jewish women.

6. There is a distinct difference in the _____ and the _____.

In fact, 1 Corinthians 14:34 where the King James Version says "women keep silent" is not an accurate translation. The word translated women is the Greek word gune; however, it can also be translated wives. With that in mind, Paul wrote 1 Corinthians 14:34 to say, "let your [gune] keep silent." But considering the very next verse says, "if they will learn anything, let them ask their husband's at home." Obviously, he was speaking about the wives who were being disruptive.

These verses were isolated cases dealing with specific situations in specific churches about a group and culture of people whose particular female segment was unlearned.

Paul was instructing the most organized and systematic way to get rid of that inequality and bring the women up in their learning to the place where they were functioning equally in the church.

In essence, Paul was saying, "We need to get these women on the same level even though society has kept them ignorant and unlearned. Teach them at home, men. We don't need to be interrupting the whole church service to do this because we've got business to take care of but be teaching them at home so there is equality and equal level of learning. Then they can be an integral part of the church."

❦ HEIRS TOGETHER ❦

1 Peter 3:7

Likewise, ye husbands, dwell with them according to knowledge, giving honor unto the wife, as unto the weaker vessel, and as being heirs together of the grace of life; that your prayers be not hindered. [8] Finally, be ye all of one mind, having compassion one of another… be courteous… knowing that you are thereunto called, that you should inherit a blessing.

1. The wife is called to _____ and _____ the Word.

2. She is ordained to walk in _____, laying the _____ of the home.

3. Husbands and wives are not heirs _____ but co-heirs _____.

1 Peter 3:7

"That your prayers be not hindered"

4. To have a strong _____, you must have a strong _____ _____.

◈ GEMS FOR REFLECTION AND APPLICATION ◈

Answer each question and then discuss. Make a corresponding action plan to accomplish these things. Recheck your action plan monthly to see if you are on target. If not, adjust and keep going.

The only way you fail is if you quit.

BOTH:

Which scripture was the most impactful to each of you in the discussion of women in this chapter?

_____

_____

_____

_____

_____

_____

_____

_____

_____

_____

_____

_____

_____

CHAPTER 6

NOTES

_____

_____

_____

_____

_____

_____

_____

_____

_____

_____

_____

_____

_____

_____

_____

_____

_____

_____

_____

_____

CHAPTER 7

SUBMISSION

1. The Bible talks more about _____ _____ to
    _____ than wives submitting to husbands.

2. _____ and _____ are woven throughout the Bible for the
    entire body of Christ.

3. What does it mean when the Bible says that wives are to _____ and
    _____ to their own husbands?

4. _____ can also be translated "wives."

1 Corinthians 14:34–35

"Let your *wives* keep silence in the churches: for it is not permitted unto them to speak; but
they are commanded to be under obedience as also saith the law. And if they will learn anything,
let them ask their husbands at home: for it is a shame for women to speak in the church."

5. Paul uses the *same* word that can be translated _____ in the following verse.

1 Timothy 2,

"Let the wives learn in silence with all subjection. But I suffer not a wife to teach, nor to
usurp authority over the man."

◈ WIVES AND HUSBANDS

1. The word *man* is translated _____ as well.

An accurate translation would be:

"But I suffer not a wife to teach, nor to usurp authority over her husband, but to be in silence."

2. The subject being addressed is specifically a _____/_____
    relationship, not a _____/_____ relationship.

Ephesians 5:21,

"Submitting yourselves one to another in the fear of God."

Paul breaks down the idea of submission over the next 11 verses, beginning with verse 22, "Wives, submit yourselves unto your own husbands, as unto the Lord."

Submit hupotasso

"to subordinate, to obey, to be under obedience, put under, subdue unto, be subject to, and in subjection to." This is a combination of two root words: *hupo* and *tasso*. The root word *hupo* means "to be under, to be beneath, or to be lower than." The word *tasso* means "to arrange in an orderly manner, to assign or dispose, to determine, appoint or ordain, to set in an orderly manner."

❖ WHAT IS THE PURPOSE OF SUBMISSION?

1. The intent of wives submitting themselves to their own husbands is to _____ _____ and a _____ of _____.

2. Paul lays out the order quite clearly: Christ is the head of _____. God is the head of _____.

3. It's a _____ of _____.

❖ AS IT IS FIT IN THE LORD

Colossians 3:18

"Wives, submit yourselves unto your own husbands, as it is fit in the Lord."

1. Submit means to be _____.

2. Obey means "to hear as a subordinate, to _____ or _____ to a _____ or _____."

3. The wife is to submit to her own husband, not to _____ _____ _____.

4. This verse is addressed specifically to the wives and says to submit _____.

5. It does *not* say to the husbands: _____ your wives submit to you."

6. Christ does not _____ _____ _____ to Him.

7. This is an act of the wife's _____ _____.

Read the section about Brother Kenneth E. Hagin on bottom of page 64 in the Diamond book.

8. Wives are to submit "_____"

    and "_____."

9. What are some things that, in your opinion, would not line up with the Word, "as it is fit in the Lord."? (Ex: lying and adultry)

    _____

❖ OUR BIBLICAL CHAIN OF COMMAND

1 Corinthians 11:3

"But I would have you know that the head of every man is Christ; and the head of the woman is the man."

1. This can be translated _____ and _____.

2. God is the head of Christ who is the head of the _____ who is the head of the _____.

3. This is the _____ of _____ within the structure of the family unit as _____ by _____.

4. Most people don't think of Jesus _____ Himself to God.

John 5:30

"I can of mine own self do nothing: as I hear, I judge: and my judgment is just; because I seek not mine own will, but the will of the Father which hath sent me."

5. Jesus is not seeking _____ _____ _____ but His Father's.

6. He is placing His will under _____ to His Father's will.

Luke 22:42

"Father, if thou be willing, remove this cup from me: nevertheless, not my will, but thine, be done"

7. This is a beautiful picture of _____ _____ and _____ by Jesus to His head, the Father.

He was about to undergo horrendous torture, physical and spiritual death, but He (of His own choosing and His own will) submitted Himself to His spiritual head, His Father.

❖ JUST LIKE JESUS

Philippians 2:5

Let this mind be in you, which was also in Christ Jesus, who, being in the form of God, thought it not robbery to be equal with God."

Philippians 2:7

"But made himself of no reputation, and took upon him the form of a servant, and was made in the likeness of men: And being found in fashion as a man, he humbled himself, and became obedient unto death, even the death of the cross."

1. Jesus _____ Himself to the will of God and took the form of a _____.

2. Two additional descriptions included in the words translated *submission* are "_____ and _____."

In 1 Peter 3 and Ephesians 5, that word *servant* is contained in the definitions of those words *submit* and *obey* as well.

3. This is _____ how Jesus operated in relation to His head, the Father God.

4. Paul explained the _____ of _____ in this manner: the head of Christ is God, the head of man is Christ, the head of the wife is the husband.

◈ HEAD OF THE HOUSE

1. Nowhere in the Bible does it say that the _____ is the _____ of the _____.

2. It says he is the head of his _____, *not* the house.

1 Timothy 5:14

"I will therefore that the younger women marry, bear children, guide the house, give none occasion to the adversary to speak reproachfully."

3. He also told him that it was _____ _____ who should be the heads and rulers of the family.

According to *Strong's Concordance,* the Greek word that is translated as "guide the house" is *oiko-despoteo* and literally means "to be the head of (i.e. rule) a family."

This is supported by the authority structure we just saw laid out by God through Paul.

4. God is the _____ of Christ, Christ is the _____ of the man, the husband is the _____ of the wife, the wife is the _____ of the house.

When Jesus was raised from the dead and God raised Him to be the head of the Church, He turned around and gave us all of His authority to rule the earth and have dominion over it, bringing it into subjection to the Word.

5. Husbands, as the heads of their wives, should give their wives _____ _____ and _____ to rule the household and bring it into subjection to the Word of God!

◈ EVEN AS SARAH...

We have looked at 1 Peter 3 a couple of times, but we skipped over something important. Every time we go back, we gain more knowledge which is exactly what 1 Peter talks about: "to dwell with them according to knowledge." We see things in a different light when we have more knowledge.

1 Peter 3:5–6

"For after this manner in the old time the holy women also, who trusted in God, adorned themselves, being in subjection unto their own husbands: Even as Sarah..."

Genesis 16:1

"Now Sarai, Abram's wife bare him no children: and she had a handmaid, an Egyptian, whose name was Hagar. Sarai said unto Abram, Behold now, the Lord hath restrained me from bearing. I pray thee, go in unto my maid; it may be that I may obtain children by her. And Abram hearkened to the voice of Sarai. And Sarai Abram's wife took Hagar her maid the Egyptian, after Abram had dwelt ten years in the land of Canaan and gave her to her husband Abram to be his wife. And he went in unto Hagar, and she conceived: and when she saw that she had conceived, her mistress was despised in her eyes."

1. Sarah mistakenly placed the _____ on _____ for "restraining her from bearing."

2. Sarah did not _____ in _____.

3. She did not stand on what the Lord _____ _____.

Genesis 16:5

"Sarai said unto Abram, My wrong be upon thee: I have given my maid into thy bosom; and when she saw that she had conceived, I was despised in her eyes: the Lord judge between me and thee. But Abram said unto Sarai, Behold, thy maid is in thine hand; do to her as it pleases you. And when Sarai dealt hardly with her, she fled from her face."

4. In other words, Sarai said to Abram, "That's what you get for being _____ _____!"

Throughout chapters 16–21, there was strife between Sarah, her maid, and Abraham. Then they added kids in the mix. What a mess! The exciting conclusion takes place in

Genesis 21:10–12

"Wherefore she said unto Abraham, Cast out this bondwoman and her son: for the son of this bondwoman shall not be heir with my son, even with Isaac. And the thing was very grievous in Abraham's sight because of his son. And God said unto Abraham, Let it not be grievous in your sight because of the lad, and because of the bondwoman; in all that Sarah hath said unto you, hearken unto her voice; for in Isaac shall thy seed be called."

5. Sarah made a _____.

6. Even though Abraham _____ and was _____, he did what she asked.

7. God _____ Sarah.

8. Sarah had plenty of _____ in the house and was not _____ _____.

Even though she made the original mistake, she went to Abraham and asked him to step in and fix it.

She stood her ground knowing that it was God's perfect plan for the promise to come through Isaac.

❧ WOMEN OF FAITH

1 Peter 3

1. Sarah is used as an example in 1 Peter 3 as a holy woman who _____ God.

2. These women had _____! They walked in faith and _____ God.

3. These women also "_____ _____, being in subjection unto their own husbands."

4. They _____ to _____ their own husbands.

❧ EXTREME REVERENCE

1. They obeyed their husbands as unto the Lord, as it was fit in the Lord, and they had _____ _____.

2. "Even as Sarah _____ Abraham, calling him lord."

3. The word *lord* is used like a surname and can also mean _____ or _____.

4. The Lord set it up for women to have _____ _____ for their husbands.

5. What if your husband isn't worthy of reverence? Remember, these were _____ of _____.

💎 ACT LIKE GOD

1. If your husband doesn't seem worthy, act like God _____ _____.

2. Treat him like he _____ the extreme reverence that you give him.

💎 FAITH AND FEAR CAN'T DWELL TOGETHER

1. Sarah did not call Abraham *lord* out of _____.

2. She was a woman of faith who _____ _____ and was not afraid of her husband.

3. Sarah _____ _____ to Abraham when she needed to and called him out on things that weren't right.

4. She had deep _____ and _____ for her husband.

5. It is no problem submitting to someone you _____, just as Jesus submitted to God because of the _____ and _____ He gave.

6. God set it up for the wife to _____, and for the husband to be _____ of her submission by _____ _____ with the Word of God.

❖ Gems For Reflection And Application ❖

Answer each question and then discuss. Make a corresponding action plan to accomplish these things. Recheck your action plan monthly to see if you are on target. If not, adjust and keep going. *The only way you fail is if you quit.*

MEN:

Is there anything you can think of that has made it difficult for your wife to submit to you?

What can you do to make it easier for her to submit to you?

_____

_____

_____

_____

_____

_____

_____

_____

WOMEN:

When were times that you have had trouble submitting to your husband in the past? Why?

What, in your life and in his, would make it easier to submit to your husband?

_____

_____

_____

_____

_____

_____

_____

CHAPTER 7
NOTES

_____

_____

_____

_____

_____

_____

_____

_____

_____

_____

_____

_____

_____

_____

_____

_____

_____

_____

_____

_____

_____

_____

_____

_____

_____

_____

_____

_____

_____

_____

_____

_____

_____

_____

_____

_____

_____

_____

_____

_____

_____

CHAPTER 8
TO THE HUSBANDS

The book of Ephesians, Chapter 5, has 10 verses dealing with the husband's responsibility to love their wives. Only three verses specifically talk about the wives submitting to their husbands.

1. Men are to _____ and _____ their wives as Christ _____ and _____ the Church.

2. That is a _____ _____ for husbands to understand.

❤ JESUS SETS AN EXAMPLE OF SUBMISSION

Philippians 2:5

"Let this mind be in you, which was also in Christ Jesus: Who, being in the form of God, thought it not robbery to be equal with God."

1. The Son _____ to God the Father.

Philippians 2:7-8

He "made himself of no reputation, and took upon him the form of a servant, and was made in the likeness of men: And being found in fashion as a man, he humbled himself." He submitted Himself by becoming "obedient unto death, even the death of the cross"

2. As an _____ of His _____, Jesus submitted Himself unto His God.

These verses demonstrate what we saw Jesus saying in the last chapter.

See Luke 22:42

"If there's any way, let this cup pass nevertheless not my will, but your will."

3. He _____ to the will of _____ _____ .

❖ WHAT HAPPENS AS A RESULT OF SUBMISSION?

1. Observe what His Head did when Jesus _____:

Philippians 2:9

"Wherefore God also hath highly exalted him, and given him a name which is above every name"

Let's review what the Word says in 1 Corinthians 11

2. God is the _____ of Christ; Christ is the _____ of man; the husband is the _____ of the wife.

3. Jesus _____ _____ to God; God raised Him up and gave Him _____ _____.

4. In the same way, when the wife submits herself to the husband, what should the husband do? _____

5. The wife submits herself of her own _____ _____ to her _____.

6. Her her head raises her up and says, "Yes, you are _____ in this _____."

Keep that principle firmly in your mind as we continue.

❖ THE BLESSING

1. The husband is to _____ to the wife as Jesus, the Head of the Church _____ to the Church.

Hebrews 7:24

"But this man because he continueth ever, hath an unchangeable priesthood. Wherefore he is able also to save them to the uttermost that come unto God by him, seeing he ever liveth to make intercession for them." That is what Jesus is doing right now for the Church! He ever liveth to make intercession for us.

Luke 24:50,

"And he [Jesus] led them out as far as to Bethany, and he lifted up his hands, and blessed them. And it came to pass, while he blessed them, he was parted from them, and carried up into heaven."

2. Jesus is forever our _____ _____ after the order of Melchizedek.

3. It is His job and responsibility to _____ and _____ the blessing on the Church.

4. This is not _____ blessing but _____ blessing!

5. A blessing might be a car, for example, but *the blessing* is the _____ _____ released by God that _____ the car.

We are using this specific example because it goes line-upon-line, precept-upon-precept, hand-in-hand with one of the few instructions to husbands contained within our foundation scripture of Proverbs 31.

6. Proverbs 31 is almost entirely about the virtuous woman _____ her household.

7. The only verse describing what the husband does is that he _____ in her.

He sits and visits with the elders at the gates (v. 23), and "her children rise up and call her blessed. Her husband also and he praises her" (v. 28).

8. One of the things that the husband is supposed to do is _____ his wife _____.

9. He should be _____ and _____ the blessing over her, just as we saw Jesus do with the Church in Luke 24.

I encourage you to study the topic of the blessing further because this is essential for husbands in knowing how we are supposed to treat our wives. There are excellent books out there on the blessing. Brother Kenneth Copeland has one called The Blessing of the Lord: It Maketh Rich and He Adds No Sorrow With It. I highly recommend this book! Read it. Study it. Research it. Find out what the blessing does because this is what you are supposed to be declaring over your wife.

◈ Intercession And Blessing

1. Jesus constantly makes _____ for us and _____ us.

2. Therefore, you should constantly make _____ declaring the _____ over your wife.

Starting at the beginning in Genesis 1, God had just finished creating the animals and the fish. Then He created man, but before He was finished He had one more thing to do. Verse 28 tells us the blessing God gave, "And God blessed them and God said unto them, Be fruitful, and multiply, and replenish the earth, and subdue it: and have dominion over the fish of the sea, and over the fowl of the air, and over every living thing that moves upon the earth." That is the blessing of God!

3. Up until that time, God looked at what He created and said "it was _____" (vv. 4, 10, 12, 18, 21, 25),

4. but after man was created and the blessing given, He called it " _____ _____" (v. 31).

We see the blessing over and over throughout scripture. In Genesis 9, mankind had come to the point where God had to start over again. So, after the flood, the only living people on the planet were Noah and his family. What did He do?

Genesis 9:1-2

"And God blessed Noah and his sons, and said unto them, Be fruitful, and multiply, and replenish the earth. And the fear of you and the dread of you shall be upon every beast of the earth, and upon every fowl of the air, upon all that moveth upon the earth, and upon all the fishes of the sea; into your hand are they delivered"

5. God _____ the _____ in the earth and released the blessing into Noah and his family.

Genesis 12:1–3

"Now the Lord had said unto Abram get thee out of thy country, and from thy kindred, and from thy father's house, unto a land that I will shew thee: And I will make of thee a great nation, and I will bless you, and make your name great; and you shalt be a blessing: And I will bless them that bless thee, and curse him that curseth thee: and in thee shall all families of the earth be blessed."

6. You can trace the blessing all through scripture to see _____ _____.

Genesis 17:6

"And I will make thee exceeding fruitful, and I will make nations of thee, and kings shall come out of thee. And I will establish my covenant between me and thee and thy seed."

7. The _____ _____, "I will make thee exceeding fruitful," from verse 6 is repeated again in chapters 26 and 28.

8. The blessing _____ _____ in the Old Testament.

Galatians 3:13

"Christ hath redeemed us from the curse of the law, being made a curse for us: for it is written, Cursed is every one that hangeth on a tree: That the blessing of Abraham might come on the Gentiles through Jesus Christ; that we might receive the promise of the Spirit through faith."

9. He tells us plainly that the whole reason Jesus came to earth was to get the _____ _____ to people!

10. He ever lives to _____ and _____ that blessing over the Church!

❖ HUSBANDS

1. Are you _____ the _____ over your wife?

2. Are you _____ releasing your faith into words of blessing over her to raise her up into a position of _____ and _____ over your home and over your household, under _____ prayer and praise?

3. That's what _____ _____ for Jesus and for us.

4. Keep in mind our _____ between Christ and man, and the husband and wife as you read the next couple verses.

Ephesians 1:22–23

God "hath put all things under [Jesus] feet and gave him to be *the head* over all things to the church, which is his body" (italics added).

Ephesians 2:6

God "hath raised us up together and made us sit together in heavenly places in Christ Jesus."

5. Jesus _____ _____ to God.

6. As His head, God turned around and _____ Him, _____ Him a name which is above every name, _____ Him up to sit with Him in heavenly places.

7. _____ _____ _____ to Christ, and God _____ us up together with Christ, _____ us with Him and His authority in heavenly places.

8. This joint heirship with Jesus (see Romans 8:17) is one of the primary factors needed so "that your _____ be _____ _____ " (1 Peter 3:7).

9. _____ submitted Himself to God and _____ exalted Him.

10. _____ submit ourselves to Christ and we have been _____ _____ together with Christ and seated with Him.

11. As the head of our wives, we husbands are to turn around and _____ _____ _____ in the household, with equal authority as joint-heirs together in this life!

❤ PRAISE HER!

Proverbs 31:28

"Her children arise up, and call her blessed; her husband also, and he praiseth her."

1. Along with declaring the blessing over her, we are to _____ our _____ .

"Good job, honey," once every six months or so is not going to cut it.

2. The word *praise* contains the meaning " _____."

3. Make it clear to your wife and everyone around _____ _____ she means to you and how _____ she is to you.

4. The word *praise* means "_____ _____." (like a diamond!)

5. You are to make it clear that she _____ in your life and in your home.

6. It also means " _____."

7. It is the _____ _____ to polish that diamond, to make her shine like a show piece.

8. Draw the _____ and _____ out of her.

9. There's a stigma with the term "_____ _____" and the _____ of women.

10. But there's a _____ _____ of that concept that is valid and biblical.

WIVES:

Your husband wants to show you off, boast about you, brag on you, show off the shining diamond in his life. This is not a sexist thing – it is a God thing!

◆ TIME TO CELEBRATE

1. Praise also means "to be _____ _____."

2. You should be a _____ for your wife's love.

3. _____ your _____!

4. Celebrate your _____ _____.

Sing her praises. Okay, for some of us, our literal singing may not be a wonderful sound, but sing the praises of your diamond. All of those concepts are contained in that one small word praiseth. Not only are you to praise God. You are to praise your virtuous wife.

◈ NOURISH HER

1 Corinthians 7:1–5

"Now concerning the things whereof ye wrote unto me: It is good for a man not to touch a woman. Nevertheless, to avoid fornication, let every man have his own wife, and let every woman have her own husband."

1. The words _____ and _____ could also be translation _____ and _____.

2. The word *have* is _____ on both parts.

3. "Let the husband render unto the wife due benevolence,"

4. Benevolence means conjugal duties. Notice it is _____ _____ listed first.

Vs 4-5

"And likewise also the wife unto the husband. The wife hath not power of her own body, but the husband: and likewise also the husband has not power of his own body, but the wife. Defraud you not one the other, except it be with consent for a time, that you may give yourselves to fasting and prayer; and come together again, that Satan tempt you not for your incontinency."

5. This is dealing with the _____ _____ between a husband and wife.

Vs 4

"The wife has not power of her own body."

6. Power also mean _____.

7. The husband has the _____ and _____ to pray for his wife's healing, physical protection, and deliverance on a level that _____.

Example:

Not too long after Lynn and I had gotten married that we were at a friend's house and spent most of the day there. Toward evening, Lynn became extremely sick. In a matter of minutes, she became delirious and was at the point of passing out. I prayed earnestly over her and heard in my spirit the first line of Psalm 23, "The Lord is my Shepard, I shall not want."

I leaned over and whispered it in her ear as she was slumped against the wall.

She told me later that when she first heard that line, it sounded far off in the distance but then it was like the rest of Psalm 23 exploded in her entire being so loudly that it was all consuming.

Within a matter of fifteen or twenty minutes, she was entirely whole and thinking clearly just as if nothing happened!

I prayed and interceded as the head of my wife and the Lord gave me His Words. They came through me into her to save, heal, and deliver her body over which I had authority! That's a picture of how this system works.

Ephesians 5:23

"For the husband is the head of the wife, even as Christ is the head of the church: and he is the savior of the body."

That word *savior* is actually the same word that's used throughout scripture to describe Jesus as our Savior, and the root word, *sozo,* is the same used as *salvation* in

Romans 10:10

"With the heart man believeth unto righteousness and with the mouth confession is made unto salvation."

8. It means _____, _____, _____, _____, and _____.

9. These are the things that the _____ is to be for _____ _____.

10. The husband is not the wife's _____ _____.

11. He has _____ over her _____.

12. He has more _____ and _____ than anyone else to pray for her healing, protection, deliverance, etc.

Ephesians 5:29

"For no man ever yet hated his own flesh; but nourisheth and cherisheth it, even as the Lord the church."

13. The word *nourish* means "to _____ up, to _____ up, to _____ up."

14. This is what the husband is supposed to do for his wife. He _____ her up and _____ her.

15. He does so through _____ the _____ over her and living to intercede praises on her behalf.

◈ BE THE ANCHOR

Ephesians 5:23

"For the husband is the head of the wife, even as Christ is the head of the church: and he is the savior of the body."

1. Let's look at the Greek word and definition of the English word _____.

2. This word means "something to be _____ upon."

3. In other words, the head is an _____ and _____.

Example:

My wife has become skilled over time through training with various elite, tactical units around the world. She is vastly more qualified than most men in protecting and defending her home and those she loves! Seeing that I do a tremendous amount of traveling with the ministry, this has always been a distinct advantage in our home.

Once when my son, Ryan, was about 5 years old, I was out of town and the kids got to sleep in my place in the bed which was something they looked forward to with great joy! One night in the early hours of the morning, there was a loud noise that woke both my wife and my son up, which was significant in Ryan's case! They both recognized the noise as someone trying to gain entrance to our home.

So Lynn instructed Ryan where to hide for safety. She took possession of her firearm and proceeded to "clear" the house.

This being done, she returned to the bedroom where our son was ready with a question. "Mom, what would you have done if someone had broken into our home?"

Lynn said, *"No one is going to endanger my children, Ryan. I would have shot them."*

Ryan continued, *"Would you have just tried to wound them or something?"*

"No, son, I would have killed them."

Ryan breathed a big sigh of relief, *"Okay, good!"* And he promptly went back to sleeping soundly again. He had the reassurance that he was well-protected by love.

I told you that story because it shows how confident my children were in Lynn's ability to protect them and the home. Yet anytime I return from a trip, they all immediately start yawning and getting sleepy! It is such a funny phenomenon. My wife laughs and says, *"I know it seems funny to you, but we all feel so much more at peace and safe when you are home. You bring such stability and steadfastness to the family."* Then she expresses those sentiments in a little more intimate detail later in the evening!

This is what the husband is supposed to be: the anchor and the stabilizer for his wife.

◈ SPECIFIC TO YOUR WIFE

GUYS:

Ask the Holy Spirit to show you how to walk these things out in practical ways specifically for your wife.

Every woman is different. You dwell with your wife according to knowledge, so you know her better than anyone. There are things that will mean more to her than they would to another woman. Be led by the spirit and walk these things out practically.

If you do, I can pretty much guarantee two things.

Number one, she will not have any problem whatsoever submitting to you and your authority over her. Having the type of respect and honor for you that Sarah of old did when she called Abraham "lord" or "master" will not be a problem because you've given her someone to respect.

Number two, the subject matter being discussed in 1 Corinthians 7:1–5 will indeed be a wonderful and glorious part of your marriage.

❖ GEMS FOR REFLECTION AND APPLICATION ❖

Answer each question and then discuss. Make a corresponding action plan to accomplish these things. Recheck your action plan monthly to see if you are on target. If not, adjust and keep going. *The only way you fail is if you quit.*

MEN:

How can you be an anchor or stabilizer to your wife?

_____

_____

_____

_____

_____

_____

_____

_____

_____

WOMEN:

What are some things your husband has done that helped stabilize you?

_____

_____

_____

_____

_____

_____

_____

_____

CHAPTER 8
NOTES

CHAPTER 9
THE RICH WIFE

This study has perhaps killed a few sacred cows, so we might as well knock a few more right between the eyes. Maybe we can finally wipe out this whole devil-inspired herd of religious lies!

1. The wife's _____ _____ is far more precious than rubies or pearls.

2. Her immense value is based on her _____ _____ and who she is _____ by God to be.

❖ ANOTHER ASPECT OF THE DIAMOND

1. This aspect is interwoven in almost every description of her in scripture that it is part of her _____ _____.

2. The wife is to be _____ _____ and _____ _____ in goods and material things.

3. She is supposed to live in _____ and have _____ things.

4. These riches and luxury are not all up to the _____.

5. Our foundation passage of Proverbs 31 lists many things about the wife that indicate _____ _____, and _____.

6. The definition of *virtuous* includes "_____ and _____, _____, _____, and _____."

7. Proverbs 31:14 says that the virtuous woman _____ and her family eats _____ _____ .

Proverbs 31:15 *AMPC*

"She rises while it is yet night and gets [spiritual] food for her household and assigns her maids their tasks".

8. V 21

   She has maids and servants who are well taken care of and well-dressed

◈ THIS WIFE IS QUITE BUSY

1. V. 16

   _____ different fields, _____ different plots of real estate,

   then _____ the properties that make good business sense

2. V. 18

   She has good, quality _____

3. V. 24

   that she makes of fine linens and _____

4. V. 20

   She is _____ and has plenty to give to the needy

5. Just as it says in 2 Corinthians 9:8, God makes _____ _____
   abound toward her so that she has _____ in all things and is able to
   abound to every good work.

◈ SHE AND HER HOUSEHOLD ARE WELL-CLOTHED

1. V. 21

   She's not afraid of the winter or hard seasons because her whole _____
   is well-clothed

2. V. 22

   As is she with _____, expensive clothing of silk and purple

In the culture and climate of that day, those fabrics and colors were exceedingly expensive items.

3. The point is she has great _____ _____,
   _____ _____, and takes care of herself.

❧ THIS WOMAN IS WEALTHY AND PROSPEROUS!

Proverbs 18:22

"Whoso findeth a wife findeth a good thing, and obtaineth favor of the Lord"

1. The word *good* in its definition denotes "_____, _____, and _____."

Proverbs 19:14

"A prudent wife is from the Lord."

2. The definition of *prudent* includes "to _____ and to have good _____."

The gemstones in Isaiah 54 are not just _____ gemstones.

Psalm 112:3

"wealth and riches are in [the righteous man's] house."

3. The _____ of the righteous man's household laid his foundations.

4. In those foundations were _____ and _____!

❧ WOMEN SUPPORTED JESUS' MINISTRY WITH THEIR WEALTH

Luke 8:1–3 *TPT*

"And also a number of women who had been healed of many illnesses under his ministry and set free from demonic power. Jesus had cast out seven demons from one woman. Her name was Mary Magdalene…Among the women were Susanna and Joanna, the wife of Chusa, who managed King Herod's household. Many other women who supported Jesus' ministry from their own personal finances also traveled with him"

The Message translation says they "used their considerable means to provide for the company"

1. These women gave of their _____ _____ to support Jesus's ministry and those who traveled with him!

2. It was _____ personal finances, not their _____.

3. These ladies were _____ _____ _____ women.

Acts 16:14

"And a certain woman named Lydia, a seller of purple..."

4. In those days the seller of purple was almost equal in wealth to _____ because purple was so rare and expensive that only nobility was allowed to wear it.

5. As a seller of purple, Lydia was a very _____ _____.

Acts 16:15

"And when she was baptized, and her household, she besought us, saying, if ye have judged me to be faithful to the Lord, come into my house, and live there. And she constrained us".

6. In that culture and time, this meant she _____ for _____!

Paul and his company lived quite well, moving into the home of a man and woman as wealthy as nobility.

7. Lydia was a _____ _____ who was generous with her _____ _____ .

Deuteronomy 19:15

...at the mouth of two witnesses, or at the mouth of three witnesses, shall the matter be established.

8. God's plan for wives to be _____ has been well _____!

❧ GEMS FOR REFLECTION AND APPLICATION ❧

Answer each question and then discuss. Make a corresponding action plan to accomplish these things. Recheck your action plan monthly to see if you are on target. If not, adjust and keep going. *The only way you fail is if you quit.*

BOTH:

What are some financial goals you want to set for your family?

_____

_____

_____

_____

_____

_____

What are some scriptures to stand on to achieve those goals?

_____

_____

_____

_____

_____

_____

What are some corresponding action steps you can take towards those goals?

_____

_____

_____

_____

_____

_____

CHAPTER 9
NOTES

_____

_____

_____

_____

_____

_____

_____

_____

_____

_____

_____

_____

_____

_____

_____

_____

_____

_____

_____

_____

_____

_____

_____

_____

_____

_____

_____

_____

_____

_____

_____

_____

_____

_____

_____

_____

_____

_____

_____

_____

_____

_____

_____

CHAPTER 10
THE WIFE—THE WARRIOR

We have explored many facets of the virtuous woman, but there is one more I want to dig into deeper.

1. The virtuous woman is _____,

2. She is _____ and _____ to her husband.

3. This woman is _____ and _____.

4. But now I want you to see that she is also a _____.

The term virtuous woman is seen again in Proverbs 12:4 using the Hebrew word *chayil*.

The word *chayil* describes a _____ _____ and is used throughout scripture.

Judges 6:12

"The Lord is with thee, thou mighty man of valor."

The word _____ is the exact same Hebrew word *chayil* translated as _____ in Proverbs 12:4 and Proverbs 31:10.

◈ THE SAME WORD

1. The description of the mighty man of valor in Judges 6 is the same as the _____ _____.

2. V. 14

    This man of valor or virtue is able to go in his might and save the entire nation of Israel

3. V. 16

    and even wipe out the all the Midianites as one virtuous man

Joshua 1:14

"But you shall pass before your brethren armed, all the mighty men of valor and help them."

4. God uses the _____ _____ as the virtuous woman to talk about the mighty men going into battle.

2 Chronicles 17:13,18

"The men of war, mighty men of valour, were in Jerusalem...prepared for the war."

5. All through here the words *virtue* and *valor* are the _____ _____.

6. Proverbs 12:4 continues to say, "A virtuous woman is a _____ to her husband."

7. The Lord used the word *virtuous* to describe women here because the Hebrew word for crown is *atarah* meaning "to _____ for _____ or _____."

Proverbs 31:11–12,17

"The heart of her husband doth safely trust in her, so that he shall have no need of spoil. She will do him good and not evil all the days of her life....She girdeth her loins with strength, and strengtheneth her arms."

8. When a husband has a genuine diamond in _____ _____ in his household of faith–one who _____ who she is, he does not need to worry about a thing.

♥ THIS IS OUR GOAL

One of our favorite movies is *Mr. and Mrs. Smith*.

The main characters are a husband and wife, who were special agents in opposing agencies before they became married but didn't know it. They are both excellent in their field of tactical expertise.

Their agencies find out they are married, and their new mission is to take each other out. But in the process, the Smiths discover that they are, in fact, truly in love. So, they decide to stand together as it should be. In the climactic scene of the movie, they face astronomical odds, outnumbered beyond belief, but they stand together. When the dust settles, the enemy is defeated and dead. And there Mr. and Mrs. Smith are, husband and wife, back-to-back, standing strong.

1. This is what _____ _____ in _____ should see when they think about coming up agains _____, your family, or your _____.

2. They don't stand a chance of defeating you when the diamond in your household knows _____ _____ _____ and is in her place, *and* the husband _____ _____ _____ because he knows it as well.

◈ GEMS FOR REFLECTION AND APPLICATION

Answer each question and then discuss. Make a corresponding action plan to accomplish these things. Recheck your action plan monthly to see if you are on target. If not, adjust and keep going. *The only way you fail is if you quit.*

MEN:

What are some examples of when you have seen your wife's fighting spirit and fierce determination?

_____

_____

_____

_____

What did you admire most about that?

_____

_____

_____

_____

WOMEN:

What are some of the things in your life that you see as valuable enough to fight for?

_____

_____

_____

_____

Are you one of those? Are your marriage and family?

_____

_____

_____

_____

CHAPTER 10
NOTES

CHAPTER 11
THE POWER OF TOGETHERNESS

Let's read these verses all together, keeping in mind the principles we've learned, and help solidify this picture in your mind:

"Submitting yourselves one to another in the fear of God, let everyone of you in particular so love his wife even as himself, and the wife see that she reverences her husband. Nevertheless, neither is the man without the woman. Neither the woman without the man in the Lord. For as the woman is of the man, even so is the man also by the woman but all things of God. Let every man have his own wife, and let every woman have her own husband. Let the husband render unto the wife due benevolence and likewise also the wife unto the husband. The wife has not power over her own body but the husband, and likewise also the husband has not power of his own body but the wife. Defraud you not one the other. There is neither Jew nor Greek, there is neither bond nor free, there is neither male nor female, for you are all one in Christ Jesus. And if you be Christ's, then are you Abraham's seed and heirs according to the promise. Marriage is honorable in all. It is valuable. Marriage is esteemed. Marriage is precious. Marriage is very pricey. And it should be held in esteem especially of the highest degree. And as being heirs together of the grace of life that your prayers be not hindered."

1. There is great _____ that the husband and wife have together.

2. It is not about one _____ another.

3. It does not include one _____ and _____ about the other.

4. The _____ of _____ is tremendous.

A number of years ago, Lynn began experiencing a multitude of physical symptoms including extreme fatigue, joint pain, sensitivity to noise and a lot of other miscellaneous and seemingly unrelated issues. Shortly after she began noticing them, she also began experiencing significant mental challenges. She wasn't able to complete sentences or think of even simple words like fork or shoe when she was trying to say them. She had extreme brain fog. Over the course of several years, it progressed to the point where if she came downstairs in the morning to vacuum the living room, she would have to stay in bed the rest of the day due to extreme exhaustion.

This type of thing is extremely rare around our home! Normally, if some physical issue arises, we pray while standing on our promises of healing contained in the Word and the issue disappears. So, needless to say, after several years of Lynn's health challenges getting worse, I sought the Lord and purposefully listened for the answer to this serious sickness.

◈ ESSENTIAL INSTRUCTIONS

1. Never question if it is God's will for _____ to take place.

2. Never entertain the idea that it _____ _____ be working.

3. Cast all the _____ and _____ of the situation onto the Lord.

4. Having done all to stand—_____ _____.

5. Keep listening for both spiritual instructions and natural, physical instructions.

I know that is easier said than done. When your wife is bed-bound for the day after brief activity and can't figure out how to say common words, it takes some diligence not to let your mind worry about the situation but it must be done!

But that is another teaching.

Anyway, we kept doing "business as usual" as much as she was physically able just as if she was healed and whole. In what seemed unrelated, someone asked us to research a set of symptoms that their wife was experiencing. Our background is in the medical field, so from time to time we are asked medical questions. I was busy with other things, so I asked Lynn to research it for me.

You have to remember that even through all of this I maintained my normal travel schedule and she kept the home running to the best of her ability including homeschooling our daughter! She had plenty of reasons to tell me "no", but she didn't. She took her place as my helpmate submitting herself to me as her head.

Well, I didn't realize it was anything miraculous. I didn't have any idea that the wisdom of God was about to be revealed! I was just praying and making supplication for my wife continually in the Spirit and doing what I was supposed to be doing. Lynn had no inclination that she was about to unlock the secret of what we had been searching for—for years at this point. She simply was doing what was right.

In the course of researching these other symptoms, she stumbled across an article about Lyme disease. She began researching the disease and discovered it included just about every symptom she had been suffering from for the last several years. In looking further into it, we found out that one of the leading Lyme disease specialists in the country lived in a town near us.

Lynn was tested and her results were positive for Lyme disease. Once we knew what it was, we pursued natural treatment but attacked it with the Word of God at the same time. She was pronounced completely free from that demonic disease in half the normal time! She is back to full function, healed and whole!

6. The _____ _____ when we do what we are supposed to do.

7. At that time, the Lord is able to get the answer to you and _____ _____ _____!

8. Thanks be to God Who _____ causes us to triumph in Him!

❖ ONE BODY

Romans 12:4–8

"For as we have many members in one body, and all members have not the same office: So we, being many, are one body in Christ, and every one members one of another. Having then gifts differing according to the grace that is given to us, whether prophecy, let us prophesy according to the proportion of faith; Or ministry, let us wait on our ministering: or he that teacheth, on teaching." The gift of each member depends upon the anointing, grace, and calling.

Ephesians 4:7, 15

"But unto every one of us is given grace according to the measure of the gift of Christ... But speaking the truth in love, may grow up into him in all things, which is the head even Christ: From whom the whole body fitly joined together and compacted by that which every joint supplies".

Matthew 19:4-6

"Have ye not read, that he which made them at the beginning made them male and female...For this cause shall a man leave father and mother, and shall cleave to his wife: and they twain shall be one flesh? Wherefore they are no more twain, but one flesh. What therefore God hath joined together, let not man put asunder"

1. The word translated _____ is literally _____.

2. Your _____ is a body—_____ body.

❧ WHAT HAPPENS IF THE JOINTS ARE OUT OF PLACE IN THE BODY?

1. What is the only time in history when Jesus' physical body was sick and diseased?

   _____

Psalm 22 begins with "My God, my God, why have you forsaken me?" and ends with "it is finished" (*AMPC*).

2. This _____ _____ describes Jesus as his physical body was dying a severely painful death

Psalm 22:14-15

"I am poured out like water, and all my bones are out of joint: my heart is like wax; it is melted in the midst of my bowels. My strength is dried up like a potsherd; and my tongue cleaveth to my jaws; and thou hast brought me into the dust of death."

Of all the things He could have described about His dysfunctional, dying body, it is significant that He said, "All my bones are out of joint."

3. This can be applied to the _____ of _____ at large and the _____ of the Church.

4. It also applies to the body of your _____ relationship!

5. _____ _____ *must* function in their particular place and grace!

6. Just as in Jesus' physical body, when the _____ are out of place in your marriage, the _____ of your marriage will be sick.

7. Your marriage body may be in pain, diseased or even so _____ that it is at the point of no longer being able to function. *But...*

When each member is in their place "according to the effectual working in the measure of every part, maketh increase of the body unto the edifying of itself in love;"

❖ KEYS TO ENJOYING A LIFE AS HEIRS TOGETHER:

1. The diamond in your household of faith knows who and what she is.

2. She understands her God-ordained and assigned position and abilities.

3. Her husband truly understands her abilities and position and gets out of her way.

4. He places the highest level of esteem and value possible on his virtuous diamond with which the Lord has blessed him.

5. He also understands his place and grace....

❖ THREE ARE EVEN BETTER

Deuteronomy 32:30

For one shall put a thousand to flight but two shall put ten-thousand to flight.

Matthew 18:20

Because where two or three are gathered together in Jesus' name, then God is in the midst of it.

1. Now you have the wife, the husband, and the "_____"—all together.

Ecclesiastes 4:12 *TLB*

A person standing alone can be attacked and defeated, but two can stand back-to-back and conquer.

The *Contemporary English Version* says it this way, "Someone might be able to beat up one of you, but not both of you.

As the saying goes, 'A rope made from three strands of cord is hard to break.'"

It's Mr. and Mrs. Smith plus the Almighty God!

2. It is time for the diamond to live out Isaiah 54. Build that foundation by _____ with the Lord, putting His _____ in your _____.

3. _____ your territory and _____ your home.

4. _____, diamond, _____.

ISAIAH 54
WEETER EXPANDED
TRANSLATION

In Isaiah 54, the Lord is talking to the _____.

Utilizing the definitions of the words and expounding on each meaning, here is what Isaiah 54 means:

"I swear a most solemn oath to you that no matter what you have been through or are dealing with now, I will not be angry with you or rebuke or yell at you. I promise you that even if the mountains would disappear, and there would be no more hills, still my kindness toward you would be in full force. Not only that but my blood sworn oath to you for my peace will always be intact and I will never break it for I have great, never-ending mercy toward you my daughter!

"You may have been attacked and treated terribly. You may have been pounded with one wave of life right after another, over and over. Just as you recovered from one thing, another came along and knocked you off your feet, pulling you under until you felt like your were drowning all throughout your life. You may have been told your entire life that you're no good and will never amount to anything, without one comforting word being spoken to you.

"But look here and let me show you what I'm going to do through you going forward!

"I am going to make you a diamond in your very own home! If you will allow Me, I will fashion and form you into a most exquisite, multifaceted diamond of the highest quality, cut, and clarity. You will have such clarity that you will be able to see how to use various other gems and elements that I will show you to build your dream home full of wealth and riches. I am personally going to set you securely and steadfastly in your setting so as to bring out your maximum shine and brilliance!

"You and I are going to sit down together and I am going to personally share My wisdom, insight, and understanding with you. I am going to show you how to build the most beautiful and successful life and home that you can imagine. You will have to do the building, but don't worry, I have the master plans and blueprints showing you exactly what to do every step of the way.

"I will give you the words that you will use to lay the very foundations of your home, raise up the walls, and install the windows! You will use the power and authority in My words by declaring them to build impregnable gates and borders that no enemy can breach. I'll show you how to mark your territory. You will indelibly engrave your borders and gates with My mark with your declarations and then defend our territory with whatever firepower necessary to overcome any foe who would dare attempt to enter without your permission.

"I have equipped you with everything needed to build your home in such a manner to where it is an impenetrable fortress. Don't misunderstand me, oppression, fear, and terror will still bluster and blow around on the outside. Lions will still roam around trying to find a way in, but if you will listen to me, I will show you how to stand firm and give you the weapons to forcefully keep them out.

"Don't be worried if you forget something I've said or you didn't listen and you get a crack in a gate or border through which an enemy is able to get in to your home. If you just stay with me and keep listening, I can fix any breech and deal with any attack at any time. I am not only your Father, I am Almighty God!

"Not only will I make your home, through you, the ultimate fortress against your enemies but it will be such a safe haven for your family. Once everything is in place, you will teach your children how to do the same thing. You will teach them of Me and how to commune with Me and I will teach them the things of the Kingdom just as I have with you. I will see to it that your children have great peace, great financial abundance, great health, long life, and great success throughout their lives in every area!

"You are My own daughter who has chosen to serve Me and this is your heritage and inheritance!"

❖ GEMS FOR REFLECTION AND APPLICATION ❖

Answer each question and then discuss. Make a corresponding action plan to accomplish these things. Recheck your action plan monthly to see if you are on target. If not, adjust and keep going. *The only way you fail is if you quit.*

BOTH:

What are some things that you have allowed to get you "out of joint" or out of agreement?

_____

_____

_____

_____

_____

_____

_____

_____

BOTH:

How can you change that in the future?

_____

_____

_____

_____

_____

_____

_____

_____

CHAPTER 11

NOTES

_____

_____

_____

_____

_____

_____

_____

_____

_____

_____

_____

_____

_____

_____

_____

_____

_____

_____

_____

CONFESSIONS AND PRAYERS

As we saw throughout this book, it is extremely important to declare and pray over your spouse in faith! This principle is set forth in Mark 11:22–25:

"And Jesus answering saith unto them, Have faith in God. For verily I say unto you, That whosoever shall say unto this mountain, Be thou removed, and be thou cast into the sea; and shall not doubt in his heart, but shall believe that those things which he saith shall come to pass; he shall have whatsoever he saith. Therefore I say unto you, What things soever ye desire, when ye pray, believe that ye receive them, and ye shall have them. And when ye stand praying, forgive, if ye have ought against any: that your Father also which is in heaven may forgive you your trespasses."

In keeping with this vital principle and tool in your endeavor to improve your marriage relationship or maintain the outstanding one you already have, I have provided you with scriptural confessions and prayers to utilize. The Word of God is, after all, medicine to your flesh—your body—and applied daily for maintenance care and three times a day for a dysfunctional body. If symptoms worsen, double the dosage! I hope you get my point.

❤ LOVE

This should be confessed in faith twice: First, placing "I" in the blanks, then again with your spouses' name placed there!

_____ endures long and is patient and kind; _____ never is envious nor boils over with jealousy, is not boastful or vainglorious, does not display myself/herself/himself haughtily. _____ is not conceited (arrogant and inflated with pride); _____ is not rude (unmannerly) and does not act unbecomingly. _____ does not insist on my/her/his own rights or my/her/his own way, for I/she/he is not self-seeking; I/she/he is not touchy or fretful or resentful; I/she/he takes no account of the evil done to me/her/him [pays no attention to a suffered wrong]. _____ does not rejoice at injustice and unrighteousness, but rejoices when right and truth prevail. _____ bears up under anything and everything that comes, is ever ready to believe the best of every person, my/her/

his hopes are fadeless under all circumstances, and I/she/he endures everything [without weakening]. _____ never fails [never fades out or becomes obsolete or comes to an end]. (1 Corinthians 13:4–8 *AMPC*)

I cease not to give thanks for _____, making mention of her/him in my prayers; that the God of our Lord Jesus Christ, the Father of glory, may give unto them the spirit of wisdom and revelation in the knowledge of him: The eyes of their understanding being enlightened; that they may know what is the hope of his calling, and what the riches of the glory of his inheritance in the saints, and what is the exceeding greatness of his power toward _____, according to the working of his mighty power, which he wrought in Christ, when he raised him from the dead, and set him at his own right hand in the heavenly places and hath raised _____ up together, and made her/him sit together in heavenly places in Christ Jesus: Far above all principality, and power, and might, and dominion, and every name that is named, not only in this world, but also in that which is to come: And hath put all things under _____ feet, and gave Jesus to be the head over all things to _____ , which is his body, the fulness of him that filleth all in all. And right now the God of peace, that brought again from the dead our Lord Jesus, that great shepherd of the sheep, through the blood of the everlasting covenant, makes _____ perfect in every good work which

God predestined (planned beforehand) for her/him [taking paths which He prepared ahead of time], that they should walk in them [living the good life which He prearranged and made ready for them to live], to do his will, working in them that which is well-pleasing in his sight, through Jesus and through His anointing; to whom be glory for ever and ever. Amen. (Ephesians 1:15–23, Hebrews 13:20–21, Ephesians 2:10 *AMPC*)

I do not cease to pray for _____ and to desire that she/he might be filled with the knowledge of God's will in all wisdom and spiritual understanding; that she/he might walk worthy of the Lord unto all pleasing, being fruitful in every good work, and increasing in the knowledge of God; strengthened with all might, according to his glorious power, unto all patience and longsuffering with joyfulness; giving thanks unto the Father, which hath made her/him able to be partakers of the inheritance of the saints in light: Who hath delivered her/him from the power of darkness, and has translated her/him into the kingdom of his dear Son: In whom they have redemption through his blood, even the forgiveness of sins. (Colossians 1:9–14)

◈ THE HUSBAND'S BLESSING DECLARATION

In taking my place and role as the head of my wife, I declare over you, _____, be fruitful and multiply and replenish this household! Subdue it and have dominion over everything in this home! Take your place as the diamond in this household of faith and build this home under the instructions and directions of the Master Builder. In doing so, all of the manifestations of the blessing will come on you and overtake you.

Blessed shall you be in the city and blessed shall you be in the field. Blessed shall be the fruit of your body and the fruit of your ground and the fruit of your beasts, the increase of your cattle and the young of your flock. Blessed shall be your basket and your kneading trough. Blessed shall you be when you come in and blessed shall you be when you go out. The Lord shall cause your enemies who rise up against you to be defeated before your face; they shall come out against you one way and flee before you seven ways.

The Lord shall command the blessing upon you in your storehouse and in all that you undertake. And He will bless you in the land which the Lord your God gives you. The Lord will establish you as a people holy to Himself. And all people of the earth shall see that you are called by the name [and in the presence of] the Lord, and they shall be in awe of you and afraid of you. And the Lord shall make you have a surplus of prosperity, through the fruit of your body, of your livestock, and of your ground, in the land which the Lord swore to your fathers to give you. The Lord shall open to you His good treasury, the heavens, to give the rain of your land in its season and to bless all the work of your hands; and you shall lend to many nations, but you shall not borrow. And the Lord shall make you the head, and not the tail; and you shall be above only, and you shall not be beneath. (Deuteronomy 28:3– 13 *AMPC*)

OR WRITE YOUR OWN
FAITH CONFESSIONS

_____

_____

_____

_____

_____

_____

_____

_____

_____

_____

_____

_____

_____

_____

_____

_____

_____

_____

_____

_____

Confessions and Prayers

Confessions and Prayers

_____

_____

_____

_____

_____

_____

_____

_____

_____

_____

_____

_____

_____

_____

_____

_____

_____

_____

_____

115

_____
_____
_____
_____
_____
_____
_____
_____
_____
_____
_____
_____
_____
_____
_____
_____
_____
_____
_____
_____

ANSWER KEY

◈

GEMSTONES

1. God created diamonds as examples of extreme **beauty,** combined with extreme **strength.**

2. A diamond's value, preciousness and rarity are **far above rubies.**

3. **Her value (price) is far above rubies.**

4. The **virtuous woman** is the **diamond** in your household of faith.

5. If the value of a diamond is far above the value of all the other gemstones, we can infer the diamond is **over all** the other gems.

6. **Your home and your household.**

7. What is the master gem in your household? Your **diamond.**

8. The Lord furnishes your diamond with **gems** to build a household.

THE SETTING

1. **Enhance the stone's brilliance**

2. **Egyptian women applied powdered antimony as make-up to enhance the eyes.**

3. The second purpose of a jewel's setting is a **Functional purpose**

4. The appropriate setting keeps the stone **secure** in its **location.**

PROPER PLACE IN THE HOME

1. **Great shall be the peace and undisturbed composure of your children; establish yourself in righteousness; far from oppression or destruction, shall not fear.**

2. What setting will enhance the diamond's **brilliance** and keep it **secure?**

3. In other words, what is the proper place in the **home** for the **wife?**

4. Due to the natural order in the physical realm on this earth, the **husband** is placed as the **head** and **covering** of his **wife.**

5. **Leader, covering, protector**

6. As we study, it becomes that the wife is at the head of the **functioning** of the **home.**

7. Essentially a family is an institution of humans that has to be **organized.**

8. Because of the multitude of **logistical issues** in a family that need to be dealt with, a wife must be **multifaceted.**

◈ CHAPTER 2: PROVERBS 31 WOMAN

PROVERBS 31:10-31 *KJV*

1. **"chaste, timid, quiet, meek, godly, pious, soft-spoken."**

2. Which language was used to write the book of Proverbs? **Hebrew**

4. **Valor**

5. "a **force,** whether of men, means or other resources; an **army, wealthy, virtue, valor, strength, able,** activity, army, a band of soldiers, or a company; great forces, goods, host, might, power, riches, strength, strong, substance, train as in training of a soldier, valiant, valor, virtuous, war, and worthy."

HOW GOD DESCRIBES THIS VIRTUOUS WOMAN

1. a. You can **trust** someone who is **worthy** and full of **valor** and **strength.**

1. b. This virtuous woman is **powerful.**

2. **God says** the Proverbs 31 woman has the means, resources, and ability to do these things.

3. She is **rich, successful** and **hard-working.**

4. She is **strong** and is not **afraid** of anything.

5. She makes **good choices** and does things with **excellence.**

6. She gives **generously** to the poor.

7. In the context of the day, these were **exquisite, fine** articles.

8. This is the description of the **ideal family** as God intended.

9. She knows how to **turn** a **profit.**

10. Her fashion style is her own, based on **strength** and **honor**

11. The virtuous woman can speak a word from God in your life and **change things.**

12. Her husband lifts her up and **praises** her! He doesn't **deride** or **embarrass** her.

13. These are the daughters taught by a virtuous woman. Elder women are to **teach** the **younger** according to the book of Titus. (See Titus 2:3–4).

14. Not only will the virtuous woman who fears the Lord have **favor** and **beauty,** but she shall also be praised.

15. She is **multifaceted** and therefore **highly valuable.**

❖ CHAPTER 3: THE REST OF THE STORY

ISAIAH 54:1-17 *KJV*

1. a. The woman described in Isaiah 54 has experienced a great amount of **pressure** and **distress.**

1. b. Even as a young wife, she was **refused**

2. The Lord has shown **mercy** and has **redeemed** her.

3. No matter what this woman has been through, the Lord can use her to **build** something **beautiful!**

THE STONES

1. As the diamond in the household of faith, the **wife** builds with the precious stones at the **Lord's instruction.**

2. The Lord will "set" them in such a way that it will show the world their **brilliance** and **shine.**

THE FOUNDATION

1. Diamonds are the **foundation** of their home.

2. Who established the diamond as such? **God**

3. Who is laying the foundations of your family? **God**

4. The wife (diamond) is to **inscribe** the foundations of the home by **declaring** the Word of God over them

5. Diamonds **mark** their homes in the **spirit,** keeping it off limits to the devil.

THE WINDOWS

1. Your diamond should have **deep,** clear **vision** for her family and the call of God on their lives.

2. The greater the clarity of the diamond, the **higher** the **value.**

3. This clarity of vision is a "notched space of battlement" through which to **overcome** all the **attacks** of the **enemy.**

THE GATES

1. The diamond is the **gatekeeper** of your home.

2. a. **Pray in the spirit.**

2. b. **Hear from God.**

2. c. **Be aware of what is trying to come into your home.**

2. d. **Decide whether something enters your home or whether it does not.**

3. a. **Functionally**

3. b. **Spiritually**

4. The idea of building the home is **reinforced.**

5. When the enemy is trying to gain access to your home, it is necessary to be a **fiery gatekeeper.**

THE BORDERS

1. A border is "a boundary, a territory **enclosed;** to bound as with a **rope.**"

2. And a three-stranded rope is not **easily broken.** (See Ecc. 4:12.)

3. The three stranded rope includes **God, husband, wife**

4. What is the border that will enclose your territory? **Three stranded rope**

5. Mark your territory? **Speak the Word of God over it.**

BUILDING EXCELLENCE

1. Once these things are in place and your home is built **securely,** these things shall take place.

2. Your home is established in **righteousness.**

3. **Oppression, fear,** and **terror** shall not come near you because your home is built well.

4. Be the **diamond** in your household of faith.

WHO IS BUILDING YOUR HOME?

1. The Lord is the **builder.**

2. He ordains everything for the **house** to be **built.**

3. The "**subcontractor**" handles all of the **labor.**

4. **Women** are the subcontractors.

5. They build the home using the **blueprints** the **Master Builder** has laid out.

6. Even if some things have gone wrong, God can and will **repair** the household of faith.

7. When the diamond builds her house with the Master Builder, it is **steadfast, strong** and **secure.**

8. So where is the diamond's place in the **building process**?

9. God gave us His Word as the **blueprint** to **build** our **household.**

THE WHOLE PICTURE

1. The sapphire is used to scratch other substances and to make a **mark** for record.

2. The wife lays the **foundation,** marking the substances around the household by **declaring,** speaking, **talking,** and **writing.**

3. The diamond **sits down together** with the Father, **gets His Words,** and she declares them, speaks them, talks about them, and marks her household off limits to Satan.

◆ CHAPTER 4: ONE WORD FROM GOD

1. Now that you have seen what the diamond of your household looks like, is a wife automatically this diamond? **No**

2. How are these scriptures obtained and implemented? **by faith**

3. Not every woman is **virtuous.**

4. Not every wife is a **good thing.**

5. In **one word,** the Lord shows the most wonderful, glorious description of the **facets** of a **wife.**

6. Whoever finds a wife, finds a **good thing.**

7. A **virtuous** wife is a **prudent** wife.

8. A prudent wife is **from the Lord.**

THE WORD WEAVES PIECES TOGETHER

1. To have understanding or to make to understand is **wisdom.**

2. A prudent wife has wisdom to **teach** and to be **successful.**

3. a. **prudence**

3. b. **goodness**

4. Implement these biblical descriptions by faith and you will become a **diamond.**

◈ CHAPTER 5: YOUR NEW FILTER

1. Keep these words with their full meanings as a **filter** through which you read scriptures regarding wives.

2. What is the traditional way of thinking about women?

   meek, mousy, pious, quiet, wimpy.

3. Don't let religious tradition **blind you** and cause you to **slip back** into the old traditional way of thinking.

4. **Renew** your **mind,** to the virtuous woman, the good wife, the prudent wife.

WIVES OF UNBELIEVING HUSBANDS

2. The household is built by **declaring** and **talking** the Word.

3. By her **success, strength, prosperity, excellence,** and **ability** to run the household well, responsibly, and efficiently, a virtuous, prudent and good wife is going to win over her unbe lieving husband.

ADORNMENT OF THE HEART

1. **Outward adornment** is only one part; the **renewing** of the **inward man** is also important to God.

2. It is the wife's **responsibility** to adorn herself in **submission** to her own husband.

3. How she looks and what **she wears** or **doesn't wear** is between the wife and her husband—and nobody else.

4. We have no right to **judge** or **speak against** someone else.

5. The wife is "of **great price,**" or far more valuable than rubies or other gemstones.

6. She is indeed the **diamond** in your household of faith.

7. "Great price" can also mean "**extremely expensive.**"

8. She is of **great value** in the sight of God.

9. In God's eyes, even compared to streets of gold and pearl gates, your wife is of **great value.**

10. A wife is **God's own daughter**!

GIVING HONOR TO

1. A wife is not the **weaker vessel.** She is **strong** and **capable.**

2. A husband is to honor her **as if** she were a weaker vessel.

3. Giving her **honor** means "to **value** as extremely costly and extremely pricey."

4. You have been given a **gift** that God sees as extremely valuable and costly.

5. If you take that gift and **treat** it with little to no **value,** how do you expect your prayers to be fully active, powerful, or effective?

6. You must sit down **together** so that your prayers be not **hindered.**

7. Husbands and wives are **heirs together** in the grace of life.

8. **Realize** who the diamond in your household of faith is.

9. Take a moment to acknowledge exactly how **valuable** and of **great price** a wife truly is in your life.

◆ CHAPTER 6: TAKING IT TO THE NEW TESTAMENT

1. In the Old Testament who should build the house? **The wife**

2. In the New Testament we will see how the **Master Builder** builds His house!

BACK TO THE FOUNDATION

1. This is the **Master Builder's** pattern—His **blueprint.**

2. It is how **Jesus** operated, and how the **diamond** should operate.

3. As He speaks His words, the **Father** does the work of laying the foundations of the home through the **diamond.**

4. Another meaning of the word foundation in Ephesians 5 and Isaiah 54 is to **teach** or to **instruct.**

5. Satan has been able to rob the households of faith and the Church by **keeping** the **woman** of the house away from being able to **teach.**

WHO IS THE SCRIPTURE REFERRING TO?

1. The same Greek word translated as "women" also means "**wives.**"

2. This verse is speaking about **husbands,** so "woman" is referring to "**wives.**"

3. It is important to take the time to **stop, study** and **research** what the words meant.

4. In Brother Hagin's book, The Woman Question, the Law of **Scriptural Interpretation** is presented.

5. In the Strong's Concordance, it shows that she speaks and teaches **wisdom**!

6. The very nature of a virtuous woman includes not only **speaking** but also **teaching.**

7. The Lord is the Master Builder and He builds the home through the **diamond.**

8. He does the teaching **through** her.

9. The definition of prudent includes the meaning "**to instruct.**"

10. A prudent wife is to **instruct!**

11. How does **faith** come?

12. That it is specifically the **spoken word**—rhema in the Greek.

13. Timothy heard the **spoken Word** of **God** from his grandmother and from his mother!

THE WORD SAYS WOMEN ARE SUPPOSED TO TEACH

1. Scripture after scripture says that women are **supposed** to **teach.**

2. Anna served God in the church, **speaking** to all who were looking for redemption.

3. A prophetess **speaks** the Word of the Lord.

4. Priscilla **taught** and **expounded** the way of God to Apollos alongside her husband.

5. It is **God-ordained** for the diamond to teach and expound the things of God in the home and even outside of it.

6. As we saw in the word **foundation,** it is an integral part of her **purpose.**

DIFFERENCES BETWEEN THE CULTURES

Greek and Roman Cultures

1. There is a **difference** between Jewish women and the Gentiles to whom Paul preached.

2. With research, you'll find that the women in the Greek and Roman cultures were kept **quite ignorant.**

3. Some women would **blurt things** out in the middle of the church service that had nothing to do with the service.

4. Paul had a systematical and organized approach to address the **disruptive behavior** and achieve **equality.**

Jewish Culture

1. Every instance we have looked at in Scripture where the women were teaching and speaking the Word of the Lord, including the prophetess Anna and Timothy's mother and grandmother, are examples of **Jewish women**.

2. The Jews **did not** keep their women ignorant.

3. They were **well taught** in the scriptures.

4. Deborah in Judges 4 was a **prophetess** as well as a **judge.**

5. She was a leader of the **whole Jewish nation,** obviously well-learned, as were all Jewish women.

6. There is a distinct difference in the **cultures** and the **circumstances.**

HEIRS TOGETHER

1. The wife is called to **teach** and **speak** the Word.

2. She is ordained to walk in **power,** laying the **foundations** of the home.

3. Husbands and wives are not heirs **alone** but co-heirs **together.**

4. To have a strong **household,** you must have a strong **prayer life.**

❧ CHAPTER 7: SUBMISSION

1. The Bible talks more about **submitting one** to **another** than wives submitting to husbands.

2. **Submission** and **obedience** are woven throughout the Bible for the entire body of Christ.

3. What does it mean when the Bible says that wives are to **obey** and **submit** to their own husbands?

4. **Women** can also be translated "wives."

5. Paul uses the same word that can be translated **wives** in the following verse.

WIVES AND HUSBANDS

1. The word man is translated **husband** as well.

2. The subject being addressed is specifically a **wife/husband** relationship, not a **woman/man** relationship.

WHAT IS THE PURPOSE OF SUBMISSION?

1. The intent of wives submitting themselves to their own husbands is to **establish order** and a **chain** of **command.**

2. Paul lays out the order quite clearly: Christ is the head of **man.** God is the head of **Christ.**

3. It's a **chain** of **command.**

AS IT IS FIT IN THE LORD

1. Submit means to be **under.**

2. Obey means "to hear as a subordinate, to **heed** or **conform** to a **command** or **authority.**"

3. The wife is to submit to her own husband, not to **any other man.**

4. This verse is addressed specifically to the wives and says to submit **yourselves.**

5. It does not say to the husbands: **Make** your wives submit to you."

6. Christ does not **make us submit** to Him.

7. This is an act of the wife's **own will**.

8. Wives are to submit "**as unto the Lord**" and "**as it is fit in the Lord.**"

9. There are many answers to this question. The most important thing is to know that the Word of God comes first. Submission does not require wives to blindly do whatever their husband tells them, especially if it violates the Word of God.

OUR BIBLICAL CHAIN OF COMMAND

1. This can be translated **wife** and **husband.**

2. God is the head of Christ who is the head of the **husband** who is the head of the **wife.**

3. This is the **chain** of **command** within the structure of the family unit as **designed** by **God.**

4. Most people don't think of Jesus **submitting** Himself to God.

5. Jesus is not seeking **His own will** but His Father's.

6. He is placing His will under **subjection** to His Father's will.

7. This is a beautiful picture of **complete submission** and **obedience** by Jesus to His head, the Father.

JUST LIKE JESUS

1. Jesus **submitted** Himself to the will of God and took the form of a **servant**.

2. Two additional descriptions included in the words translated submission are "**slave** and **servant.**"

3. This is **exactly** how Jesus operated in relation to His head, the Father God.

4. Paul explained the **chain** of **command** in this manner: the head of Christ is God, the head of man is Christ, the head of the wife is the husband.

HEAD OF THE HOUSE

1. Nowhere in the Bible does it say that the **man** is the **head** of the **house**.

2. It says he is the head of his **wife**, not the house.

3. He also told him that it was **young women** who should be the heads and rulers of the family.

4. God is the **head** of Christ, Christ is the **head** of the man, the husband is the **head** of the wife, the wife is the **head** of the house.

5. Husbands, as the heads of their wives, should give their wives **complete authority** and **power** to rule the household and bring it into subjection to the Word of God!

EVEN AS SARAH...

1. Sarah mistakenly placed the **blame** on **God** for "restraining her from bearing."

2. Sarah did not **walk** in **faith**.

3. She did not stand on what the Lord **had promised**.

4. In other words, Sarai said to Abram, "That's what you get for being **my head!**"

5. Sarah made a **demand**.

6. Even though Abraham **disagreed** and was **grieved**, he did what she asked.

7. God **backed** Sarah.

8. Sarah had plenty of **authority** in the house and was not **blindly submissive**.

WOMEN OF FAITH

1. Sarah is used as an example in 1 Peter 3 as a holy woman who **trusted** God.

2. These women had **faith**! They walked in faith and **trusted** God.

3. These women also "**adorned themselves**, being in subjection unto their own husbands."

4. They **dressed** to **please** their own husbands.

EXTREME REVERENCE

1. They obeyed their husbands as unto the Lord, as it was fit in the Lord, and they had **extreme reverence**.

2. "Even as Sarah **obeyed** Abraham, calling him lord."

3. The word lord is used like a surname and can also mean **master** or **sir**.

4. The Lord set it up for women to have **extreme reverence** for their husbands.

5. What if your husband isn't worthy of reverence? Remember, these were **women** of **faith**.

ACT LIKE GOD

1. If your husband doesn't seem worthy, act like God and **call things that be not as though they are**.

2. Treat him like he **deserves** the extreme reverence that you give him.

FAITH AND FEAR CAN'T DWELL TOGETHER

1. Sarah did not call Abraham lord out of **fear.**

2. She was a woman of faith who **trusted God** and was not afraid of her husband.

3. Sarah **stood up** to Abraham when she needed to and called him out on things that weren't right.

4. She had deep **reverence** and **respect** for her husband.

5. It is no problem submitting to someone you **respect**, just as Jesus submitted to God because of the **reverence** and **honor** He gave.

6. God set it up for the wife to **submit**, and for the husband to be **worthy** of her submission by **lining up** with the Word of God.

❖ CHAPTER 8: TO THE HUSBANDS

1. Men are to **love** and **treat** their wives as Christ **loves** and **treats** the Church.

2. That is a **foundational principle** for husbands to understand.

JESUS SETS AND EXAMPLE OF SUBMISSION

1. The Son **submitted** to God the Father.

2. As an **act** of His **will,** Jesus submitted Himself unto His God.

3. He **submitted** to the will of **His Head**.

WHAT HAPPENS AS A RESULT OF SUBMISSION?

1. Observe what His Head did when Jesus **submitted**

2. God is the **head** of Christ; Christ is the **head** of man; the husband is the **head** of the wife.

3. Jesus **submitted Himself** to God; God raised Him up and gave Him **His name**.

4. **Raise her up and give her his name.**

5. The wife submits herself of her own **free will** to her **head.**

6. Her her head raises her up and says, "Yes, you are **equal** in this **household.**"

THE BLESSING

1. The husband is to **relate** to the wife as Jesus, the Head of the Church **relates** to the Church

2. Jesus is forever our **High Priest** after the order of Melchizedek.

3. It is His job and responsibility to **declare** and **pronounce** the blessing on the Church.

4. This is not **a** blessing but **the** blessing!

5. A blessing might be a car, for example, but the blessing is the **spiritual force** released by God that **produces** the car.

6. Proverbs 31 is almost entirely about the virtuous woman **managing** her household.

7. The only verse describing what the husband does is that he **trusts** in her.

8. One of the things that the husband is supposed to do is **call** his wife b**lessed**.

9. He should be **pronouncing** and **declaring** the blessing over her, just as we saw Jesus do with the Church in Luke 24.

INTERCESSION AND BLESSING

1. Jesus constantly makes **intercession** for us and **blesses** us.

2. Therefore, you should constantly make **intercession** declaring the **blessing** over your wife.

3. Up until that time, God looked at what He created and said "it was **good**"

4. but after man was created and the blessing given, He called it "**very good**"

5. God **reestablished** the **blessing** in the earth and released the blessing into Noah and his family.

6. You can trace the blessing all through scripture to see **God's plan.**

7. The **same promise**, "I will make thee exceeding fruitful," from verse 6 is repeated again in chapters 26 and 28.

8. The blessing **doesn't stop** in the Old Testament.

9. He tells us plainly that the whole reason Jesus came to earth was to get the **blessing back** to people!

10. He ever lives to **declare** and **pronounce** that blessing over the Church!

HUSBANDS

1. Are you **declaring** the **blessing** over your wife?

2. Are you **purposely** releasing your faith into words of blessing over her to raise her up into a position of **authority** and **dominion** over your home and over your household, under **your** prayer and praise?

3. That's what **God did** for Jesus and for us.

4. Keep in mind our **comparison** between Christ and man, and the husband and wife as you read the next couple verses.

5. Jesus **submitted Himself** to God.

6. As His head, God turned around and **exalted** Him, **gave** Him a name which is above every name, **raised** Him up to sit with Him in heavenly places.

7. **We submit ourselves** to Christ, and God **raises** us up together with Christ, **seats** us with Him and His authority in heavenly places.

8. This joint heirship with Jesus (see Romans 8:17) is one of the primary factors needed so "that your **prayers** be **not hindered**" (1 Peter 3:7).

9. **Jesus** submitted Himself to God and **God** exalted Him.

10. **We** submit ourselves to Christ and we have been **raised up** together with Christ and seated with Him.

11. As the head of our wives, we husbands are to turn around and **raise them up** in the household, with equal authority as joint-heirs together in this life!

PRAISE HER!

1. Along with declaring the blessing over her, we are to **praise** our **wives**.

2. The word praise contains the meaning "**to be clear.**"

3. Make it clear to your wife and everyone around **how much** she means to you and how **valuable** she is to you.

4. The word praise means "**to shine**." (like a diamond!)

5. You are to make it clear that she **shines** in your life and in your home.

6. It also means "**to make a show**."

7. It is the **husband's job** to polish that diamond, to make her shine like a show piece.

8. Draw the **luster** and **brilliance** out of her.

9. There's a stigma with the term "**trophy wife**" and the **objectification** of women.

10. But there's a **different aspect** of that concept that is valid and biblical.

TIME TO CELEBRATE

1. Praise also means "to be **clamorously foolish**."

2. You should be a **fool** for your wife's love.

3. **Celebrate** your **diamond**!

4. Celebrate your **virtuous wife**.

NOURISH HER

1. The words **man** and **woman** could also be translation **husband** and **wife**.

2. The word have is **possessive** on both parts.

3. "Let the husband render unto the wife due benevolence,"

4. Benevolence means conjugal duties. Notice it is **his responsibility** listed first.

5. This is dealing with the **sexual relationship** between a husband and

6. Power also means **authority.**

7. The husband has the **right** and **authority** to pray for his wife's healing, physical protection, and deliverance on a level that **no one else has**.

8. It means **protection, deliverance, safety, health**, and **healing**.

9. These are the things that the **husband** is to be for **his wife.**

10. The husband is not the wife's **spiritual savior**.

11. He has **authority** over her **body.**

12. He has more **power** and **authority** than anyone else to pray for her healing, protection, deliverance, etc.

13. The word nourish means "to **bring** up, to **build** up, to **raise** up."

14. This is what the husband is supposed to do for his wife. He **builds** her up and **raises** her.

15. He does so through **declaring** the **blessing** over her and living to intercede praises on her behalf.

BE THE ANCHOR

1. Let's look at the Greek word and definition of the English word **head**

2. This word means "something to be **seized** upon."

3. In other words, the head is an **anchor** and **stabilizer**.

CHAPTER 9: THE RICH WIFE

1. The wife's **inherent value** is far more precious than rubies or pearls.

2. Her immense value is based on her **personal qualities** and who she is **designed** by God to be.

ANOTHER ASPECT OF THE DIAMOND

1. This aspect is interwoven in almost every description of her in scripture that it is part of her **spiritual DNA**.

2. The wife is to be **financially wealthy** and **very rich** in goods and material things.

3. She is supposed to live in **luxury** and have **luxurious** things.

4. These riches and luxury are not all up to the **husband**.

5. Our foundation passage of Proverbs 31 lists many things about the wife that indicate **wealth**, **riches**, and **luxury**.

6. The definition of virtuous includes "**means** and **resources**, **goods**, **riches**, and **substance**."

7. Proverbs 31:14 says that the virtuous woman **travels** and her family eats **imported food**.

THE WIFE IS QUITE BUSY

1. **Considers** different fields, **evaluates** different plots of real estate, then **buys** the properties that make good business sense

2. She has good, quality **merchandise**

3. that she makes of fine linens and **sells**

4. She is **generous** and has plenty to give to the needy

5. Just as it says in 2 Corinthians 9:8, God makes **all grace** abound toward her so that she has **sufficiency** in all things and is able to abound to every good work.

SHE AND HER HOUSEHOLD ARE WELL CLOTHED

1. She's not afraid of the winter or hard seasons because her whole **household** is well-clothed

2. As is she with **luxurious**, expensive clothing of silk and purple

3. The point is she has great **business sense**, **works hard**, and takes care of herself.

THIS WOMAN IS WEALTHY AND PROSPEROUS!

1. The word good in its definition denotes "**bountiful**, **prosperity**, and **wealth.**"

2. The definition of prudent includes "to **prosper** and to have good **success**."

   The gemstones in Isaiah 54 are not just **figurative** gemstones

3. The **diamond** of the righteous man's household laid his foundations.

4. In those foundations were **wealth** and **riches**!

WOMEN SUPPORTED JESUS' MINISTRY WITH THEIR WEALTH

1. These women gave of their **considerable means** to support Jesus's ministry and those who traveled with him!

2. It was **their** personal finances, not their **husband's**.

3. These ladies were **Proverbs 31 virtuous** women.

4. In those days the seller of purple was almost equal in wealth to **nobility** because purple was so rare and expensive that only nobility was allowed to wear it.

5. As a seller of purple, Lydia was a very **wealthy woman**.

6. In that culture and time, this meant she **paid** for **everything**!

7. Lydia was a **virtuous woman** who was generous with her **financial success**.

8. God's plan for wives to be **rich** has been **well established**!

◈ CHAPTER 10: THE WIFE—THE WARRIOR

1. The virtuous woman is **strong**

2. She is **submissive** and **equal** to her husband.

3. This woman is **rich** and **prosperous**.

4. But now I want you to see that she is also a **warrior.**

   The word chayil describes a **fierce warrior** and is used throughout scripture.

Judges 6:12

   The word **valor** is the exact same Hebrew word chayil translated as **virtuous** in Proverbs 12:4 and Proverbs 31:10.

THE SAME WORD

1. The description of the mighty man of valor in Judges 6 is the same as the **virtuous woman**.

4. God uses the **same word** as the virtuous woman to talk about the mighty men going into battle.

5. All through here the words virtue and valor are the **same word.**

6. Proverbs 12:4 continues to say, "A virtuous woman is a **crown** to her husband."

7. The Lord used the word virtuous to describe women here because the Hebrew word for crown is atarah meaning "to **encircle** for **attack** or **protection**."

8. When a husband has a genuine diamond in **her place** in his household of faith – one who **knows** who she is, he does not need to worry about a thing.

THIS IS OUR GOAL

1. This is what **every demon** in **hell** should see when they think about coming up against **you**, your family, or your **household of faith**.

2. They don't stand a chance of defeating you when the diamond in your household knows **who she is** and is in her place, and the husband **trusts in her** because he knows it as well.

◈ CHAPTER 11: THE POWER OF TOGETHERNESS

1. There is great **power** that the husband and wife have together.

2. It is not about one **dominating** another.

3. It does not include one **nagging** and **complaining** about the other.

4. The **power** of **togetherness** is tremendous.

ESSENTIAL INSTRUCTIONS

1. Never question if it is God's will for **healing** to take place.

2. Never entertain the idea that it **might** **not** be working.

3. Cast all the **worry** and **care** of the situation onto the Lord.

4. Having done all to stand—**keep** **standing**.

6. The **answer** **comes** when we do what we are supposed to do.

7. At that time, the Lord is able to get the answer to you and **provide** **total** **deliverance**!

8. Thanks be to God Who **always** causes us to triumph in Him!

ONE BODY

1. The word translated **flesh** is literally **body**.

2. Your **marriage** is a body—**one** body.

WHAT HAPPENS IF THE JOINTS ARE OUT OF PLACE IN THE BODY?

1. What is the only time in history when Jesus' physical body was sick and diseased?

   when He was on the cross-bearing sickness and disease for us!

2. This **prophetic** **psalm** describes Jesus as his physical body was dying a severely painful death

3. This can be applied to the **body** of **Christ** at large and the **functionality** of the Church.

4. It also applies to the body of your **marriage** relationship!

5. **Each** **spouse** must function in their particular place and grace!

6. Just as in Jesus' physical body, when the **joints** are out of place in your marriage, the **body** of your marriage will be sick.

7. Your marriage body may be in pain, diseased or even so **disjointed** that it is at the point of no longer being able to function. But...

THREE ARE EVEN BETTER

1. Now you have the wife, the husband, and the "**I am**"—all together

2. It is time for the diamond to live out Isaiah 54. Build that foundation by **consulting** with the Lord, putting His **declarations** in your **mouth**.

3. **Mark** your territory and **build** your home.

4. **Shine**, diamond, **shine.**

ISAIAH 54 WEETER EXPANDED TRANSLATION

In Isaiah 54, the Lord is talking to the **woman**.

www.ingramcontent.com/pod-product-compliance
Lightning Source LLC
Chambersburg PA
CBHW081656270326
41933CB00017B/3186